A GUIDE TO UNITED NATIONS
CRIMINAL POLICY

CAMBRIDGE STUDIES IN CRIMINOLOGY

A GUIDE TO
UNITED NATIONS
CRIMINAL POLICY

Manuel López-Rey

Series Editor: A.E. Bottoms

Gower

Published by
Gower Publishing Company Limited,
Gower House,
Croft Road,
Aldershot,
Hants GU11 3HR,
England.

Gower Publishing Company,
Old Post Road,
Brookfield,
Vermont 05036,
U.S.A.

ISBN: 0 566 05070 6

British Library Cataloguing in Publication Data

López-Rey, Manuel
    A guide to United Nations criminal policy.—
    (Cambridge studies in criminology; 54)
    1. United Nations   2. Crime and criminals
    I. Title   II. Series
    364   HV6030
    ISBN 0–566–05070–6

Typeset in Great Britain by
Guildford Graphics Limited, Plaistow, Nr Billingshurst, West Sussex
Printed and bound in Great Britain by
Biddles Ltd, Guildford and King's Lynn

Contents

ERRATUM
p. 41 A line has been omitted. Following line 28 the next paragraph should begin: 'The study of the following documents: *Proposed Programme Budget . . .*'

Foreword

Many people with an interest in crime policy – policymakers, administrators, academics and practitioners – are aware of the important role which the United Nations has played in this field in the post-war period, for example in the adoption of the Standard Minimum Rules for the Treatment of Prisoners, or in promoting an interest in the policy implications of the link between crime and development. The quinquennial United Nations Congresses on crime policy have always been important events.

But despite the general awareness of the importance of the UN in this field, few would claim detailed understanding of the way in which UN criminal policy has developed, or a full knowledge of the content of the policy. Hitherto an important hindrance to acquiring such an understanding has been the absence of any comprehensive single guide to UN criminal policy. It is for this reason that the *Cambridge Studies in Criminology* series is particularly glad to publish this volume by Professor Manuel López-Rey, which for the first time provides such a guide.

No-one could be better equipped to write the *Guide* than Professor López-Rey, who has been associated with UN crime policy since 1947 and still today is chairman of the UN Committee on Crime Prevention and Control. For many years Professor López-Rey has also been a Visiting Fellow of the Institute of Criminology here in Cambridge, and it is therefore a particular pleasure to be able to publish his book in the *Cambridge Studies*. I am sure that the book will reach a wide audience in many countries.

A.E. Bottoms

About the author

Manuel López-Rey was formerly County Court Judge and Professor of Criminal Law, at the University of Salamanca. From 1947 to 1966 he worked with the United Nations, first as Chief of the Section of Research and International Treaties on Narcotic Drugs and from 1952 as Chief of the Section on Prevention of Crime. Professor López-Rey has been United Nations consultant on several occassions and since 1979 a member of the Committee on Crime Prevention and Control, of which he was elected Chairman in 1984. He has published numerous papers and several books on criminological and criminal policy matters. For seventeen years he has been Visiting Professor at the Institute of Criminology, Cambridge.

Introduction

Since 1946 the United Nations has evolved a criminal policy, originally to deal with the prevention of crime and the treatment of offenders, the importance of which is greater than ever in view of what a General Assembly resolution has called 'the escalation of crime and violence in many parts of the world and the increased difficulties encountered in reducing the forms and dimensions that crime has assumed' (General Assembly resolution 36/21, 1981). The same resolution also invited member states 'to intensify their efforts to make criminal justice systems more responsive so that crime prevention and criminal justice be consonant with the principles of social justice'. Finally, as a directive, it declared that 'crime prevention and criminal justice should be considered in the context of economic development, political and social systems'. The three main conclusions to be deduced from this and previous General Assembly resolutions on criminal matters are that crime, particularly violent crime, constitutes one of the most serious problems of our time; that frequently the penal systems of the world are unable to deal with it; and that criminal justice consonant with social justice is in many countries non-existent. Certainly the conclusions may be rejected, especially by states ideologically interested in giving the impression that their penal systems function properly. Their assertions however, do not delude anyone. At present crime is one of the most salient features of contemporary society whether capitalist or not.

It is true that United Nations documents show that in some states efforts have been made to implement UN criminal policy, but for reasons which will be examined later, not all the efforts yield the results expected. In many cases they aim only at the prevention of conventional or common crime (i.e. committed by the 'man in the street'), rather than that committed by those more highly placed at the political, ideological, economic and other levels.

If one includes not only resolutions, recommendations, decisions and programmes but also notes, reports, working papers, summary records, inquiries, data, publications, etc., a conservative estimate is that no less than 4000 documents deal in different ways with UN criminal policy matters. It may be argued that 'criminal policy' matters are strictly speaking to be found only in resolutions and recommendations, but this is not always the case. Moreover, quite often recommendations and resolutions cannot be fully understood without going into the corresponding background papers in which explanations are given and difficulties of implementation dealt with. Admittedly, in some cases there is some repetition, contradiction and confusion sometimes caused by the officialese style of some documents, the main purpose of which is to encourage some governments to do more than they have done in criminal policy matters. But even if quite a number of documents are discarded (and in order to do so one has to go through all of them) the amount left is enough to justify a systematic presentation: this is the purpose of this book.

The book is based on the analysis of a large number of selected documents but does not claim to be complete; some omissions are unavoidable. However, the fundamental aspects of UN criminal policy are considered and examined for the benefit of governments, policy-makers, professionals, institutions and organizations dealing with the crime problem, including the UN Secretariat and related agencies.

The first chapter of the book is devoted to an overview of the development of UN criminal policy and in the second the machinery for putting it into effect is described and analyzed. The third chapter deals with the main subjects of the policy. The exposition mostly, but not exclusively, follows a historical trajectory which better than any other permits the appreciation of the fluctuations, trends and validity of the criminal policy evolved. The last chapter is devoted to the writer's comments and to the problems involved in making more effective that policy the implementation of which is urgent if the problem of crime is sensibly to be reduced.

The book will inform the reader of what has been done already by the UN – though sometimes forgotten, which explains why some repetitions are now presented as new; of what is being done now, often subject to opposing purposes, which is logical in view of the diversity of countries and regimes involved but illogical if the principles and purposes of the Charter are kept in mind; and finally of what may occur in the immediate future – which, unless something is done to reduce the escalation of crime, particularly that perpetrated for political, ideological and economic reasons, will offer a way of life in which freedom, equality, dignity and security will be reduced to theoretical slogans. As we will see, United Nations leadership in criminal policy is more necessary and certainly more justified than that claimed in other fields.

The book is descriptive and analytical and the analysis should not be regarded as against any UN body, government, international agency or non-governmental organization, and still less the Secretariat or the Committee on Crime Prevention and Control.

The views expressed are my own and should not be identified with those expressed by the bodies mentioned.

I wish to thank the Secretariat, particularly the Crime Prevention and Criminal Justice Branch and the Divisions of Human Rights and Narcotic Drugs for providing me with the documents requested. Also the Max-Planck Foundation for the financial assistance which enabled me to carry out research in New York, Geneva and Vienna.

For the sake of clarity notes and references have been reduced to a minimum. One of the sources which should be consulted is the *International Review of Criminal Policy,* published by the United Nations.

1 Overview

In June 1946 the UN Temporary Social Commission, later the Social Commission and at present the Commission for Social Development, decided that the prevention of crime and the treatment of offenders were part of United Nations social policy. By referring to prevention and treatment as main aims, the Temporary Commission followed the traditional criminological and criminal policy approach then prevailing in the Western world. On the other hand, by stating that both aims were part and parcel of United nations *social* policy the Commission opened the way to the present wider approach of considering crime in the context of development at the national and international levels.

The wider approach was based on the purposes and principles of the Charter in which article 55 makes specific references to stability, economic and social conditions, development, respect for human rights and fundamental freedoms, all matters closely linked to the problem of crime. The term 'development' was already used in criminal policy matters by the end of the 1950s and was regarded as a basic element of that policy at the Second United Nations Congress, held in London in 1960. Since then it has been constantly used in the formulation of UN criminal policy. The same may be said about human rights and fundamental freedoms, the criminal violation of which in many countries has increased the amount and gravity of crime and raised the question of whether crime, human rights and fundamental freedoms are so closely linked at the national and international level that at the present historical juncture it would be difficult to separate the first from the other two.

The inclusion of criminal policy matters as part of UN social policy was originally opposed by the USSR and some of her followers. (Yugoslavia, however, was always in favour of inclusion.) The reason given by the Soviet delegation was that following paragraph 7 of article 2 of the Charter the problem of crime was a domestic matter and therefore outside UN interference.[1] The objection was rejected by an overwhelming majority. Significantly it was raised at a time when the USSR was under Stalin's rule. After his death, in 1958, the Soviet Union initiated an active participation in criminal justice matters which has so far been maintained, and has often been extremely constructive.

At the outset, the Temporary Social Commission took special care that all its proposals on crime prevention and the treatment of offenders should be settled by the Social Commission and the Economic and Social Council (ECOSOC) before any consultation with the International Penal and Penitentiary Commission took place about the transfer of the functions of the latter to the UN. Such a firm and praiseworthy attitude explains why, before the transfer was accomplished, the UN had its own criminal policy programme, which as it was adopted by the Temporary Social Commission comprised the following items:

(a) the promotion by medical and educational measures of the readjustment of children with antisocial tendencies;

(b) the organization of vocational training for children leaving school and the employment and protection of such children;

(c) the treatment of juvenile offenders according to medical and educational methods by which punishment should be replaced by special measures;

(d) community organization for the prevention of crime;

(e) the promotion of probation and other methods of supervision;

(f) the consideration of questions relating to the trial, conviction and sentencing of adult offenders such as apprehension, police and social investigation, identification, detention, trial procedure, legal aid and rights of the defendant;

(g) the treatment of offenders having regard to their classification, scientific methods for the specialization of institutions, individualization of treatment in order to effect the rehabilitation of offenders and the protection of society;

(h) the study of the best methods for the organization of post-institutional treatment and after-care; and

(i) preventive action against the basic causes of delinquency and crime.

Moreover the Temporary Social Commission suggested that the functions of the League of Nations concerning the traffic of women and children, prostitution and related matters should be transferred to the UN and become part of the activities enumerated.[2]

The role of the League in criminal policy matters was rather limited. It never had a professional service of its own dealing with them, and most of what was done was delegated to some of the then existing international organizations devoted to crime problems, all of which were predominantly European. The rivalry among them was one of the obstacles faced by the League in organizing its own criminal policy unit. The vast majority of the activities undertaken referred to juvenile delinquency, and a number of studies were published. Generally, the Advisory Committee on Social Questions was in charge of the publications. In 1925 the Howard League urged the League of Nations to play a more positive role in penal and penitentiary matters; the same request was repeated by the International Federation of League of Nations Societies between 1927 and 1933 with limited results.[3]

Nevertheless, from 1933 onward the League's activities in promoting international cooperation in criminal policy matters increased with the cooperation of the international technical organizations. Several studies on fair trial matters, observance of humane prison conditions, prostitution, narcotics, etc., were distributed. The most significant was the Standard Minimum Rules for the Treatment of Prisoners prepared by the IPPC (docs. C.260.M.241,1930 and A.26 and A.44, 1933). The initial draft was transmitted in 1929 to member and non-member states. A revised text was adopted by the League in 1935 and submitted to governments, asking them to give publicity to the Rules; to ensure that the necessary steps be taken for their implementation; and to submit regular reports. Several governments sent their comments, and the analysis of these shows that the implementation of the Rules faced many difficulties, some of them of a political character. One of the comments states that the conditions in the correctional camps of the country concerned are well above the minimum proposed. For details, see doc. A.25,1936.IV which in this and other respects shows how difficult it is to ensure humane treatment of prisoners in a number of countries.

At its Second Session, also in 1947, the Social Commission studied the *Preliminary Report on the Prevention of Crime and the Treatment of Offenders* (doc. E/CN 5/30, Rev.1, 1947) prepared by the Secretariat, which may be regarded as a faithful account of what was at that time considered criminal policy. The most significant antecedents of international cooperation are also described. Apparently the first attempt took place in 1846 in Frankfurt at the International Congress of Penitentiary Science. A plan concerning prevention as well as treatment was submitted and discussed, but the European revolutionary movements from 1848 onwards prevented any positive action. In fact, the victory of the reactionary regimes increased the number of common and political prisoners almost everywhere, and governments were not interested in building up a real international cooperation for the more humane treatment of offenders.

As social defence activities, the *Preliminary Report* lists the social and non-social determinants of crime such as family problems, the formation of attitudes and habits in childhood leading to delinquency and crime, 'careers of crime', poverty, slums, alcoholism, drug addiction and commercialized vice. Concerning treatment, it stated that its main purpose was the correction of the offender, making a distinction between children, adolescents and adults. The importance of probation, the problems involved in short-term imprisonment, the distinction between institutional and non-institutional treatment, female offenders, interchange of staff, training matters and technical assistance in criminal policy were also included.

The discussion of the social defence programme took longer than expected, and it was at the Third Session of the Commission (doc. E/799,1948) that the final list was adopted. Its main subjects were: juvenile delinquency, medical and psychological examination of offenders before being sentenced, probation, fines, open institutions, habitual offenders, inquiry into the functions of medical, psychological and social sciences in the prevention of crime and the treatment of offenders, and criminal statistics. The Commission also adopted a resolution by which the Secretary-General should convene once a year a group of internationally recognized experts (not to exceed seven in number) selected by him in such a way that the group maintained an international character, in order to advise the Secretary-General and the Social Commission in devising and formulating policies in crime prevention and the treatment of offenders. In the same resolution ECOSOC was invited to declare that, in view of the importance of an international study of the prevention of crime and the treatment of offenders, the UN should assume leadership in promoting this activity, having regard to national and international organizations interested in this field. ESOSOC endorsed the opinion of the Social Commission in August 1948 by resolution 155C (VII), which, as well as declaring such leadership, requested the Secretary-General to convene in 1949 a group of internationally recognized experts as suggested by the Social Commission. In promoting its leadership, the UN should make full use of the knowledge and experience of international and national organizations which had interests and competence in the field.

The request for leadership was entirely justified in view of the growing importance of crime and the lack of an effective coordination of activities among the existing international organizations dealing with prevention and treatment. The rivalries were still going on when the UN decided to have its own criminal policy at an international level, something which could never be attained by the existing organizations.[4]

The adopted programme of social defence leaned too much towards treatment. If account is taken of the then prevailing conditions in the treatment of offenders in the vast majority of countries, including those of the Western world, it was no doubt justified. On the other hand, prevention should have received more attention, but here again the then contemporary criminology and criminal policy held the belief that by preventing juvenile delinquency crime would be considerably reduced. The reasoning is valid only as far as some types of common crime are concerned, and far less with respect to those resulting from the criminal abuse of power which will be examined in chapter 3. Such abuse of power was manifest in Western industrial society. In any case the programme should be commended since, like any other, criminal policy cannot completely ignore the existing trends at a certain historical juncture. The main problem is how and when these trends should be put aside for the more effective prevention of crime, the protection of victims and the better treatment of offenders. The matter will be examined in chapter 3. No doubt similar remarks will be made in the 1990s about the criminal policies adopted in the 1980s. Yet changes are sometimes justified, and they were made in the second part of the 1950s after the First UN Congress.

As part of this initial period, reference should be made to the transfer of the functions of the IPPC to the UN which, while beneficial, is sometimes erroneously regarded as the main point of departure of UN criminal policy. To cut a long story short, already in 1946 when the question was raised at the Temporary Social Commission it was decided that, as far as international criminal policy was concerned, the UN would always have greater resources, a larger geographical extent and would command more acceptance than the IPPC even if, as some suggested, the latter were promoted to something like an international agency linked to the UN. In spite of the resistance offered by some European members of the IPPC, the United States, as the most important member, forced the transfer.[5] It was opposed by the Soviet delegation – Russia had been an active member of the IPPC – on the grounds that 'the IPPC was a minor international organization'. The remark was unfair: it is true that geographical extent plays a role and that only 24 states (18 of them European) were members of the Commission but the importance of an international organization should also be measured by the work done, and that of the IPPC was praiseworthy. Other countries were also against the transfer because since 1946 the UN had a criminal policy of its own and from 1948 assumed international leadership. But the transfer was adopted by the General Assembly in December 1950 by resolution 415(V). The Annex to the resolution contains a plan of action mostly to be carried out by the UN which, summarily described, consists in organizing: a system of national correspondents appointed by the governments as a source of information on criminal policy matters; consultative groups of experts with a rather regional character; an ad hoc advisory committee of experts; quinquennial congresses; and the publication of an international review.[6]

It would be difficult to maintain that as a whole the system of national correspondents has yielded the results expected. For the obvious shortcomings in a number of cases neither the IPPC nor the Secretariat should be blamed. The only consultative group organized was the European, which did good work. It was mostly constituted by old members of the IPPC. The organization of the ad hoc committee had already been decided by the Social Commission, and was first convened in 1949. Undoubtedly the IPPC Congresses were the most significant precursors of UN Congresses but those organized by the UN are not 'similar to those previously organized by the IPPC' as suggested in the 1950 plan of action. The reasons for the differences are many and can be deduced from what is said about UN Congresses in chapter 2. The International Review of Criminal Policy is published in pursuance of a recommendation of the Social Commission endorsed by the ECOSOC in 1949, and in accordance with the General Assembly resolution already cited.

In the 1950s the real panorama of crime became more visible. While in the past it had been reduced, mostly under the influence of a capitalist industrial society and a conservative criminology and criminal policy, to some of the most common forms of conventional crime, the international exposure which took place in the 1940s of Nazi and other atrocities – war crimes, genocide, the widespread use of cruel, inhuman or degrading treatment of political dissidents, the frequent violation of human rights, the political and economic abuses of colonialism and institutional terrorism – showed that the problems of crime could not be confined to the consideration of conventional crime. In this respect the General Assembly resolution of 11 December 1946, the Universal Declaration of Human Rights, and the Genocide Convention opened the way for a wider consideration of the crime problem. Eventually, due mostly to the efforts of the Secretariat, this has led to the recognition of the abuse of power as one of the main sources of crime.

The rapid process of decolonization stressed the link between crime and development already latent in some of the social causes of crime, as then understood. In this respect it should be remembered that development is part of the principles and purposes of the Charter on which social defence programmes were originally based. Consequently, after some Secretariat discussions, the matter was brought before the 1953 ad hoc group of experts which recommended as one of the items of the Second Congress, in London in 1960, the Prevention of types of crime resulting from social changes and accompanying economic development in less developed countries. Some of the reasons given were that in many developing countries the penal systems have been superimposed upon the society, that in some cases this Western imposition has increased crime, and that there was a close correlation between socioeconomic development and crime.

The London Congress marks a major turning point of UN criminal policy, away from a policy markedly devoted to treatment questions and towards one of far-reaching aims based on the correlation between crime and development in which planning, as an instrumental device, is extremely important. From then on the Secretariat, the Social Commission (later the Commission for Social Development), ECOSOC, the advisory committee of experts (later the Committee on Crime Prevention and Control) and sometimes the General Assembly, stressed the significance of the correlation between crime and development as one of the tenets of UN criminal policy. Shortly thereafter the Secretariat perceived that in crime, development and planning, the role of power, sometimes beneficial and sometimes detrimental, was more often than not decisive.

There are too many documents dealing with the correlation of crime and development and planning to mention them all here. The following are cited as the most significant: ECOSOC resolution 1086B XXXIX, 1965, which stresses the integrated character of crime and socioeconomic development; the Secretariat's report *International Action in the Field of Social Defence (1966–1970)*, (E/CN 5/C.R,1966), in which it is stated that 'the prevention and control of crime and delinquency should be undertaken as part of a comprehensive economic and social development'; *Progress Report on Programmes in the Field of Social Development* (E/CN 5/409/Add.4,1967) stating that criminal policy is closely related to general social development; the Report of the Fourth Congress, in Kyoto in 1970, organized under the slogan 'Crime and Development', in which the subject of social defence policies in relation to development planning was discussed and some recommendations adopted; *A Policy Approach to Planning in Social Defence* (United Nations, 1972), somewhat disappointing since only some of the contributions actually deal with the subject, a shortcoming for which the Secretariat is not responsible; the Crime Prevention and Control Committee report, *Methods and Ways Likely to be Most Effective in Preventing Crime and Improving the Treatment of Offenders* (1977), which has been considered by some as a guideline for future activities in criminal policy matters; and the working paper *New Perspectives in Crime Prevention and Criminal Justice and Development. The Role of International Cooperation* (A/Conf.87/10,1980) submitted by the Secretariat to the Caracas Congress in which, following General Assembly resolution 32/60, 1977, it is stated that crime is hampering economic, social and cultural development, threatening the enjoyment of human rights and fundamental freedoms, and has created an increasing concern about the functioning of criminal justice systems. In addition, it is correctly stated that it is not possible to establish a general causal relationship between criminality and development because both are dynamic concepts, but that there is a growing awareness that certain changes in the socioeconomic structure and cultural patterns resulting from economic growth and social change might affect deviance and criminality. In sum, 'a better appreciation of crime trends is needed and crime prevention must be dealt with in connection with various development issues.' The most recent document is *Prevention of Crime and Criminal Justice in the context of Development* (E/AC.57/1984) in which demographic, economic, social and cultural but not political factors are examined. To these various documents should be added the articles on the subject published by the *International Review of Criminal policy*, no.25 (1967).

There is little doubt that whatever fluctuations there may be in UN criminal policy in the immediate future, crime, development, planning and power constitute a tetralogy which cannot easily be discarded. All the signs are that more and more it will become one of its main tenets. The Secretariat's initiative in trying to ascertain to what extent a New International-National Criminal Justice Order (NINCJO) may be correlated to the proposed New International Economic Order (NIEO) and vice versa confirms this.

By bringing that tetralogy to the fore, behavioural problems are not ignored. But in the present post-industrial society, in which all countries are involved in different degrees at the national and international level, the conditioning of behavioural problems cannot be interpreted as it was at the time of a conservative industrial society with its corresponding criminology, criminal justice and a series of penal reforms that never amounted to a planned criminal policy. The importance attached to development should not, however, be identified with any particular ideology according to which the economic factor plays the ultimate role in the building of the structure and superstructure of society.

This overview shows that UN criminal policy has steadily moved from treatment aims to a far larger socioeconomic, cultural and political purpose. As we will see in chapter 3, like any other policy it has not been free of hesitations, deviations, distortions and contradictions. This does not detract from its increasing importance at the national and international levels.

Notes

1. The paragraph reads as follows: 'Nothing contained in the Charter shall authorize the United Nations to intervene in matters which are essentially within the domestic jurisdiction of any state or shall require the Members to submit such matters to settlement under the present Charter, but this principle shall not prejudice the application of enforcement measures under Chapter VII'. Chapter VII deals with the functions of the Security Council concerning the threats to peace, breaches of the peace and acts of aggression which in the last 20 years imply criminal abuses of power which often should be regarded as part of UN criminal policy.
2. See *Report of the Social Commission,* First Session, 1947, (doc. E/CN 5/3,1947) which contains a detailed discussion of the proposals submitted by the Temporary Commission.
3. For details the Official Journal of the League of Nations should be consulted. In no. 115 (1933) the League thanked the technical organizations for their collaboration. The most significant were the International Penal and Penitentiary Commission, the Howard League for Penal Reform, the International Association of Penal Law, the International Association of Childrens' Court Judges and the International Bureau for the Unification of Penal Law.
4. For a list of those concerned with criminal policy matters see *International Review of Criminal Policy* (United Nations, New York), no. 1 (January 1952).
5. See *Proceedings of the IPPC* (1949 and 1950).
6. For the full text of the resolution see *International Review of Criminal Policy,* no. 1 (January 1952). At the General Assembly the representative of the Secretary-General stated that the plan did not constitute a contract and therefore alterations could be made by the Secretary-General if necessary. The statement was fully justified and was used when a few years later some European delegations said that the 'contract' had been broken by the Secretary-General when some modifications were introduced in social defence matters. Logically, the assets of the IPPC should also have been included in the transfer account taken of the assignments to be carried out by the UN even if some of them were in operation before the transfer. The assets were used to create the International Penal and Penitentiary Foundation (IPPF), which has been active internationally and has cooperated with the UN.

2 Machinery

The organizational machinery of UN criminal policy is part of the constantly growing UN family which, despite some sound advice, has not as yet found a good method of 'international agency birth-control'. To cite one example, the greatest difficulty in the formulation of a NINCJO in the context of development and the NIEO is that there are no less than 21 major international agencies dealing with development matters, most of which overlap.

The main part of the machinery for UN criminal policy is constituted by the General Assembly, ECOSOC, the Commission for Social Development, the Secretariat, some of the specialized agencies and, more specifically, the congresses, the Committee on Crime Prevention and Control (CCPC), the regional institutes and a substantial number of international and non-governmental organizations (NGOs) directly interested in penal, penitentiary, criminological and related matters.

According to article 7 of the Charter, the General Assembly, ECOSOC and the Secretariat are among the six principal UN bodies; of the other three (the Security Council, Trusteeship Council and the International Court of Justice) only the first sometimes deals with forms of criminal aggression, although the expression is seldom used.

The coining of the term 'criminal policy' has been attributed to several authors and has been in use since 1800. Criminal policy has a pragmatic character and essentially aims at the planned formulation and implementation of a policy which, within the framework of respect for human rights, is able to cope reasonably with the problem of crime. As such it should be flexibly formulated, but its pragmatic condition does not mean that it should be constantly changing or contradictory: otherwise it will lose credibility and effectiveness. The penal system is the main but not the only 'product' of a criminal policy. It should be based on a serious appraisal of national and international realities, avoid theoretical or ideological monopolies as much as possible, and refrain from unnecessary waste of efforts and financial resources. For obvious reasons, partly stated by ECOSOC resolution 155 C(VII) 1948, UN criminal policy must be flexible enough to accommodate national characteristics which are not always permanent or clearly manifest.

As we shall see, UN criminal policy is formulated by a large number of bodies and sometimes under the influence of political aims. In conformity with the definition given, it is not merely an ensemble of penal reforms, sometimes badly coordinated, at the national level. It implies not only coordination, particularly with the purposes and principles of the Charter, but also a certain continuity which does not exclude change. Changes are sometimes required, but in making them careful attention should be given to the reasons for them. Improvisation, model imitation and, above all, undue ideological allegiance should be excluded: unfortunately their exclusion is not always easy.

The General Assembly and Economic and Social Council

As a rule the General Assembly endorses or adopts what has been done by other bodies in criminal policy matters. Its adoption in 1975, on the recommendation of the Fifth Congress, of the Declaration on the Protection of All Persons from being Subjected to Torture or other Cruel, Inhuman or Degrading Treatment or Punishment is a case in point.[2] Sometimes the General Assembly takes the initiative by asking the competent body to consider a particular problem.

Examination of the large number of ECOSOC resolutions on criminal policy matters shows that sometimes it has taken the initiative in bringing in new policies, but mostly it has endorsed or adopted what has been done by subsidiary bodies or by the Congresses. Historically one of the most significant resolutions was resolution 10 (III)1946 by which, in establishing the permanent Social Commission, ECOSOC instructed it, *inter alia,* to consider how effective machinery could be developed 'for studying on a wide international basis, the means of the prevention of crime and the treatment of offenders'. As stated, the Social Commission proceeded accordingly and ECOSOC endorsed its work by adopting resolution 155 C(VII) 1948 already mentioned. In 1957 ECOSOC resolution 663 C(XXIV) approved the Standard Minimum Rules for the Treatment of Prisoners and endorsed the Recommendations on the Selection and Training of Personnel for Penal and Correctional Institutions and on Open Institutions as adopted by the First UN Congress, in Geneva in 1955. In 1975 resolution 1930(LVII) took the initiative of inviting member states to provide information on capital punishment, and requested the Secretary-General to report on practices and statutory rules which may govern the right of a person sentenced to capital punishment to petition for pardon, commutation or reprieve, and to report on these questions to ECOSOC. Moreover, as we will see later, ECOSOC has played the primary role in shaping the structure and functions of the CCPC.

Particularly active in criminal violations of human rights is the Commission of Human Rights, the effective contribution of which will be examined in chapter 3. Suffice it to say here that as far back as 1950 its excellent study, *Detention of Adults Prior to Sentence* (E/CN.5/AC.4/L, Add.1, 1950) raised the question of torture on which interesting interventions were made, some of them anticipating what has been said from 1975 onwards at the UN criminal policy level. Closely related to specific crime problems are some of the activities of the Statistical, Narcotics, Population and Transnational Commissions, the Office of the High Commissioner for Refugees, the Status of Women Commission and the Committee on an International Agreement on Illicit Payments. To them should be added other commissions and committees dealing with matters less directly affecting the problem of crime. All of them raise the question of inter-agency coordination not easily solved, about which something is said later.

The cooperation of the regional economic commissions in criminal policy is modest. The exception is the Commission for Asia and the Far East (ECAFE) which has sometimes cooperated with the UN Asian and Far East Institute (UNAFEI). In her opening statement at the CCPC meeting in Vienna in March 1982, Mrs L. Shahani, Assistant Secretary-General for Social Development and Humanitarian Affairs, stated that the involvement of the regional commissions in UN criminal policy is essential in order to maximize their impact at the regional level.

As a result of the invitation sent in 1948 by the Secretary-General in implementation of ECOSOC resolution 155 C(VII), the specialized agencies as well as the NGOs with consultative status have since then cooperated with the UN in the evolution of its criminal policy. The International Labour Office (ILO), World Health Organization (WHO) and the United Nations Educational, Scientific and Cultural Organization (UNESCO) have contributed to the study of prison labour, abnormal offenders, juvenile delinquency and violence. The number of NGOs dealing with crime problems has steadily increased since 1948.

Already in the 1950s the suggestion was made by the Secretariat and at some of the ad hoc advisory committees that in order to remedy the financial condition and at the same time improve their cooperation, some of them should amalgamate, but the suggestion was rejected. Fortunately, partly due to the efforts of the Crime Prevention and Criminal Justice Branch (hereafter referred to as the Branch), the alliance of NGOs is a positive contributing factor in the criminal policy work carried out by the Secretariat. Its *Survey of the Treatment of Foreign Prisoners* (1982), is a good contribution.[3]

Although the Security Council was never supposed to deal with criminal matters, the truth is that it does, and some of them are significant enough to warrant a place in UN criminal policy and leadership. For example, some breaches of the peace, acts of aggression, terrorism, war crimes and genocide are blatant forms of criminal abuse of power, a matter of particular importance and already discussed as part of such policy. In the perpetration of these and similar offences, states, governments, high-level civil and military officials and international political organizations are the actual offenders. The fact that the offences are labelled as crimes against the peace, war crimes, crimes against mankind, etc., does not alter their condition of common crimes committed by somebody other than the 'common man'. All constitute an ensemble of murders, bodily and mental injuries, rapes, violations of human rights, damages, etc., the distinction of which from common crime is, for political reasons, more apparent than real. Yet it is often supported juridically by weak but superficially impressive theories of international penal law. History shows that the criminal responsibility of the bodies and officials mentioned can no longer be put aside, and that the separation between national and international criminal justice is not in accordance with the demands of the concept of development in which human rights should play a primary role. As we will see, the separation of the crime problem into conventional and non-conventional crime, although useful for explanatory purposes, does not mean that as a phenomenon crime is divided into two parts. The inclusion of non-conventional crime as part of UN criminal policy has already been accepted, partly due to the efforts of the Secretariat.

The Committee on Crime Prevention and Control

The origin of the CCPC is not General Assembly resolution 415(V) 1950 but the two first ad hoc committees held in 1949 and 1950, the latter before the resolution had been adopted. Both were organized in accordance with ECOSOC resolutions 155 C(VII) 1948 and 243(IX) 1949, which endorsed the decisions of the Social Commission asking for the setting up of a group of internationally recognized experts, the advisory functions of which would be to assist the Secretary-General in the formulation and implementation of UN leadership in criminal justice. With some variations, the wording then used was incorporated into paragraph (c) of the General Assembly resolution.

The first two committees set up the following guiding principles: social defence activities should neither engage in the study of general social, economic and cultural measures directed at the improvement of conditions of living – although such measures may make an incidental contribution to the prevention of crime – nor directly engage in fundamental research into the causation of crime and delinquency, but should be devoted to the collection of information on the experience of different countries with respect to specific measures. The 1949 group understood this to mean the early detection and treatment of potential delinquents, the 'problem of the personality' (the quotation marks were used in the Report) and the prevention of recidivism. The way in which the personality question was dealt with shows that not all members of the group were in agreement. The cautious attitude of some of them has been confirmed by the way in which the personality of the offender has been put forward by numerous professionals as the main cause of crime and delinquency.

The exclusion of general social and economic questions is still valid; it has often been mentioned at regional meetings and as a rule kept in mind by the Secretariat. The Reports of the 1949 and 1950 groups of experts show that already then the relationship between general conditions and crime had been taken into account, but that by itself it was not able to provide a causal explanation of crime or, for that matter, to prevent it. The reference to avoiding causation research is fully justified in view of the impossibility of conducting it on a world-wide scale. Such exclusion does not prevent, indeed on the contrary it requires, that such research be undertaken at the national level and the results taken into consideration, provided that generalizations are avoided and any causation established is not regarded as permanent. Even within a given country the causes are not the same everywhere.

The 1949 group also recommended that in the work to be done geographical distribution should be taken into account, that the co-operation of governments should be sought as much as possible, that national working groups dealing with specific matters should be organized, and that the cooperation of international organizations interested in crime problems should be secured. Moreover, the convenience of organizing the advisory groups on a permanent basis was already raised.

One of the main features of the advisory committees before the mid-1960s was that the experts were appointed by the Secretary-General, a practice which was made official by the General Assembly which has been modified by successive resolutions, not all of them adopted by the General Assembly. Nowadays the experts are proposed by member states and appointed (in fact also selected) by ECOSOC. Which of the two systems is the best? The answer is not easy. Certainly during the first years the groups of experts made contributions which are still valuable. On the other hand, although some of them held high administrative positions, their recommendations were sometimes impractical. The governmental character of the CCPC is undeniable, but it may easily be justified by pointing out that as a sociopolitical phenomenon crime cannot be left only in the hands of experts.

The 1955 advisory group was the first which took care of the organization of congresses by dealing with the agenda and the way in which the 1955 Congress should conduct its work. Since then this has been one of the major functions of the committees which, incidentally, was not specifically mentioned by General Assembly resolution 415(V). Another significant precedent was established by the 1958 advisory group when it decided that it was within its functions to question the *Statement by the Under-Secretary for Economic and Social Affairs to the ad hoc Committee of Experts on the Prevention of Crime and the Treatment of Offenders* (E/CN.5/AC.9/R.2,1958) in which, in view of the difficulties encountered, the Under-Secretary hinted at the reduction of social defence activities. The main reason given was that crime was mostly a question affecting 'special groups' closely related to the social and welfare policies of the Department. Curiously enough, the thesis had previously been denied by the Secretary-General in his report on the *Programme of Concerted Practical Action in the Social Field* (E/CN.5/291,1953) already mentioned. As a result the reduction did not take place, although some internal Secretariat arrangements concerning the Section of Social Defence were made – all of them, fortunately, of short duration.

In its special report, *Social Defence Policies in Relation to Development Planning* (E/CN 5/C.3/R 4/Rev.1,1969) the advisory committee, which met in Rome in 1969, recommended that development planners and policy-makers should keep in mind that economic and social policies always have a crime and delinquency generating effect and that in order to reduce it adjustments should be made taking into account the problems of crime and delinquency. In 1970 the advisory committee, which met in Kyoto immediately after the Congress, recommended that social defence specialists should be trained in economic and social planning. Anticipating the successive enlargement of the committee membership, it suggested the constitution among its members of working groups or subcommittees, the contributions of which would reinforce the UN social defence programmes (E/CN.5/457,1970).

The Committee meeting held at Geneva in 1974 deserves particular attention because, following a commendable Secretariat initiative, it discussed transnational criminality and violence, thus opening up new perspectives for UN criminal policy. During the discussion references were made to the effects of rapid social and technological change and the increase of consumer fraud, corruption, new types of extortion, illegal procurement of works of art, international violence, assassinations, hijacking, kidnapping, etc., as well as to the new international jurisdictional problems raised by these and similar crimes in most of which the abuse of power, whether political, ideological or economic, was clearly visible. The term 'transnational' was defined as embracing crimes committed ouside those described by international conventions. It was stated correctly that the distinction between national, international and transnational crime was only relative and that no clear line could be drawn between the three. Concerning the so-called 'new and special types of crime' it was said that in many cases they were no more than new ways of perpetrating traditional offences.

At its meeting at Vienna in 1978 the Committee discussed the need for a better coordination of UN criminal policy activities, and heard that the restructuring of the economic and social sectors of the Secretariat also implied the setting up of closer links between the CCPC and the Commissions on Human Rights, Narcotics and Transnational Corporations as well as with all the ad hoc subcommittees dealing with terrorism, hostages and other matters clearly within the criminal policy field. As for the Secretariat, the CCPC recommended that the restructuring should give the central unit dealing with criminal policy matters a status consonant with its overall responsibility so as to be consistent with the political, juridical, humanitarian and developmental nature of the mandates involved. Briefly, the need to strengthen the coordination among all units dealing with questions directly affecting crime prevention and criminal justice was made quite clear.

During the discussions on the guidelines for crime prevention and criminal justice, it was pointed out that there was a lack of a balanced approach to the problem since the guidelines overemphasized the needs of the accused or of the offender far more than those of the community (E/CN.5/558,1978). The remark was correct and should be kept in mind in the future. It means that while the individual should not be ignored, the community should receive more attention. On the other hand, the Secretariat has been right in maintaining the title *United Nations Norms and Guidelines in Criminal Justice* instead of *Guidelines for Expeditious and Equitable Handling of Criminal Justice,* favoured by the CCPC which refers only to one aspect of the contemplated norms and guidelines.[4]

By its resolution 1979/19, of May 1979, ECOSOC, following the recommendation of the Commission for Social Development which had been suggested by the USSR, entrusted the CCPC with the preparation of the congresses; the submission to the competent UN bodies and congresses of programmes of international cooperation in crime prevention on the basis of principles of sovereign equality of states and non-interference in internal affairs; the coordination of UN activities in crime control matters; assisting the Secretary-General by submitting its findings and recommendations; the promotion of the exchange of experiences gained by the states in crime prevention and the treatment of offenders; and the discussion of major issues as a basis for international cooperation. Finally, ECO-SOC requested the Secretary-General to take all necessary measures to ensure the implementation of the resolution.

At the same session ECOSOC adopted resolution 1979/30 by which the membership of the Committee was increased from 15 to 27, geographically distributed as follows: seven seats to Africa, six to Asia, three to Eastern Europe, five to Latin America and six to Western Europe and other states. The distribution raised some well-founded objections. Certainly geographical considerations are important, and as a rule they are taken into account in the UN, but how should they be understood? Should not geographic distribution be combined with other criteria such as national effectiveness in criminal policy matters, respect for human rights, or real international cooperation? The question cannot be discussed here but suffice it to say that political geography alone is not always the best guide.[5]

When the CCPC met at Caracas in September 1980, for only five working days, it had not met since June 1978. In five days it was supposed to discuss the implementation of ECOSOC resolution 1979/19, the long-term programme of work of the Committee, the preparation of the Seventh Congress including the agenda, and the review of the rules of procedure of the congresses. No wonder then that the question of better working arrangements was discussed and given priority. The continuity of the work of the Committee during the intervening periods was raised and some suggestions made. After some discussion the Committee adopted a resolution, the main points of which were that in order to carry out its functions a list of all UN responsibilities directly related to crime prevention and control, as well as a brief assessment of the degree to which the bodies in charge of UN responsibilities are able to fulfil those assigned to them, should be prepared by the Secretariat. The request is fully justified but up to now it has not been implemented. Moreover, the Committee stressed the fact that in view of the increased mandate entrusted to it, provisions should be made to enable it, as well as the Secretariat, to fulfil the demands made, particularly those concerning 'the coordination within the various United Nations bodies and with Member States' as required by resolution 1979/19. As for the assessment of crime trends and crime prevention policies, it was stated that 'the efforts made have revealed some limitations, particularly those related to the excessive sophistication of the instrument used which had made it impossible for some countries with a limited data base to respond'. The instrument was the questionnaire sent by the Secretariat which, although technically correct, was obviously unrealistic if account is taken of the situation as regards the collection of criminal statistics in the vast majority of countries and the means they have at their disposal. In sum, with barely five working days at its disposal, and by concentrating on subjects of primary importance, among which the effectiveness of its functions was the most significant, the Committee discharged its responsibility commendably.[6]

The seventh session of the CCPC took place in Vienna in March 1982 and lasted ten working days. The agenda was: implementation of ECOSOC resolution 1979/19, the preparation of the Seventh Congress and its agenda, the revision of congress rules of procedure and arbitrary and summary executions. With the exception of the latter, all were part of the agenda of the previous session, a repetition which confirms the lack of time at the disposal of the Committee. The inclusion of the last item was in accordance with General Assembly resolution 35/172,1980.

As part of the implementation of its functions the question of whether the Committee was entitled to report directly to ECOSOC instead of reporting to the Commission for Social Development was raised again.[7] The discussions showed a contradiction between the numerous and complex functions assigned to the Committee and what is understood by functional and standing committees and expert bodies. Since 1984 the CCPC reports directly to ECOSOC.

During the general discussion on the agenda of the Seventh Congress some members did not agree with all the items or with the way in which some had been approached. This was particularly the case with the item on juvenile delinquency, eventually called 'youth, crime and justice'. The reason was that at present youth, crime and justice are part and parcel of crime prevention and criminal justice (see the section on juvenile delinquency in chapter 3). Yet owing mostly to lack of time the agenda was adopted with a few terminological changes.

At its eighth session in 1984, the CCPC was faced with a much too heavy agenda and with the fact that most of the documents for discussion were provided at the last minute by the Secretariat. The items were: revision of the rules of procedure for United Nations congresses; continuation of the preparation for the Seventh Congress; humane treatment of offenders; crime prevention and criminal justice in the context of development; women and the criminal justice system; arbitrary and summary executions; progress report on United Nations activities in crime prevention and control; consideration of the agenda for the ninth session of the CCPC and adoption of the report. All the items were supposed to be discussed in barely ten working days. Although, as in 1982, working groups were organized and the Committee worked hard, the fact remains that time was too short, that only a few documents were available in advance and that the pressure on the Committee and the Secretariat was totally unjustified. The sessions of the CCPC should be longer and the Secretariat – not only the Branch – should make arrangements to distribute all documents well in advance.

The document concerning the *Code of Conduct for Law Enforcement Officials* (E/CN.5/1984) shows that although all member states were invited to provide information about its implementation only 29 or barely 18 per cent of the membership complied with the invitation. Moreover most of the answers refer only to existing national provisions and give no factual information about their implementation. The implications of such a limited governmental reaction were not discussed. The documents concerning the preparation of the Seventh Congress required a detailed analysis and discussion which was prevented by lack of time. The same applies to crime prevention and criminal justice in the context of development and the progress report. The Committee deserves praise for the work done.

Congresses

Up to now the UN has organized six Congresses, one every five years: in Geneva (1955), London (1960), Stockholm (1965), Kyoto (1970), Geneva (1975) and Caracas (1980). The seventh will take place in Milan in 1985. All in all they confirm the effectiveness of UN leadership in criminal policy matters.

As the main instrument of UN leadership, Congresses are expected to offer practical guidance in national and international criminal policies and the bases for an effective social criminal justice at both levels. Therefore the larger their scope the greater the danger that the conclusions adopted will be too general or too numerous and fragmentary to offer the required leadership and subsequent governmental implementation. Also the way in which each Congress works is reflected in the coordination, or lack of it, between the decisions adopted.

The First Congress, in Geneva in 1955, considered the following subjects: Standard Minimum Rules for the Treatment of Prisoners; the selection, training and status of prison personnel; open penal and correctional institutions; prison labour; and the prevention of juvenile delinquency. In all, 512 persons from 61 countries and territories attended, of whom 191 were delegates representing 51 governments – at that time the number of independent countries was far smaller than it is at present. The ILO, UNESCO, WHO, the Council of Europe and the League of Arab States, as well as 43 NGOs, were represented with a total of 101 participants. The number of individual participants was 230, constituting almost 45 per cent of the total attendance.

Up to now the Standard Minimum Rules has been one of the greatest contributions ever made in criminal policy matters and the role initially played in their formulation by the IPPC should always be kept in mind. The fact that they are not fully applied depends on political, economic, social and other circumstances which not all governments are able to overcome, particularly when political instability or dictatorship prevail. The discussion of the prevention of juvenile delinquency attracted the greatest number of participants. At that time juvenile delinquency was regarded mostly as an all-embracing category in which delinquent, abandoned, orphaned, and maladjusted minors were dealt with.

In fact the agenda of the Congress reflects to some extent the continuity of past international activities in which treatment played the dominant role. The way in which the prevention of juvenile delinquency was dealt with also reflected the prevailing conceptions of Western society.

The Second Congress, in London in 1960, discussed the following items: new forms of juvenile delinquency, their origin, prevention and treatment; special police services for the prevention of juvenile delinquency; prevention of types of criminality resulting from social changes and economic development in less developed countries; short-term imprisonment; the integration of prison labour with national economies, including the remuneration of prisoners; and pre-release treatment and after-care as well as assistance to dependants of prisoners.

The number of participants was 1131, and 70 governments and 50 NGOs were represented. In addition to the specialized agencies mentioned with respect to the First Congress, the Commission for Technical Assistance in Africa South of the Sahara attended. There were 632 individual participants, a little more than 50 per cent of the whole attendance. The USSR participated in the Congress for the first time.

The debate on juvenile delinquency brought face to face the supporters of the maladjustment viewpoint adopted at the First Congress, and those who more realistically and scientifically advocated a distinction between the maladjusted and those who commit crime for other reasons, after all not all delinquents are maladjusted, and nobody is ever well-adjusted in every respect. The Congress adopted the sensible recommendation that the concept of juvenile delinquency should be reduced to violations of criminal law. With respect to economic and social changes, the coordination between national planning and the planning of crime prevention as well as the assertion that criminality may or may not be related to socioeconomic development were clearly stated. By stressing the positive and negative roles of development, the Congress laid the foundations upon which later the study of crime should be connected to development which, as it was then said, should not just be understood from the economic point of view. The pioneering work of the 1960 Congress is ignored by those who consider that the connection between crime and development was laid down in the 1970s.

The Third Congress, in Stockholm in 1965, was organized under the slogan 'Prevention of Criminality'. The items on the agenda were social change and criminality; social forces and the prevention of crime; community preventive action; measures to combat recidivism; probation, especially adult probation; and special preventive and treatment measures for young adults. In all 1083 persons attended, 74 governments and 39 NGOs were represented, as well as the Specialized Agencies which attended the previous Congresses. The number of individual participants was 658 which is a little over 60 per cent of the total.

Contrary to the previously existing practice and General Assembly resolution 415(V), the Congress did not make any recommendations or reach any conclusions. Such a negative attitude may partly be explained by the vagueness of the terms 'social forces' and 'social change' as bases for discussion. No definition of either term was ever attempted, although more than once the need was pointed out to do so in order to avoid the stream of generalizations made. The result was that under 'social forces' and 'social change' urbanization, public opinion, education, migration and many other general topics were discussed without any clear indication of their links with criminal policy. The reports of the different sections merely summarized the generalizations made.

More constructive were the views expressed when some specific topics were discussed: among them, that the official records of offenders should be improved if they were to be of any value for research; that greater attention should be given to the coordination and planning of prevention; that provided they did not mechanically copy the Western countries, the developing countries would perhaps be able to arrest by dynamic action in the mental health field a great many of the phenomena of mental disorders that beset the economically developed countries; and that the unification of the relevant services should be aimed at. All these points had a practical and policy value, and are still valid and applicable to many countries whatever their condition.

The Fourth Congress, in Kyoto in 1970, had as its slogan 'Crime and Development' and the items on the agenda were: social defence policies in relation to development planning; participation of the public in the prevention and control of crime and delinquency; the Standard Minimum Rules in the light of recent developments in the correctional field; and organization of research for policy development in social defence. In all there were 1014 participants; 85 governments were represented by 338 delegates, and 30 NGOs attended, plus the usual specialized agencies. The number of individual participants was 556, constituting more than 50 per cent of the total attendance.

The most significant conclusions were those concerning crime and development, which stressed the need for planning and the correlation of national planning with social defence planning; also that in order to achieve this, proper provision should be made in terms of information, personnel, the participation of other government agencies, and financing. Further, it was recommended that social defence planning should be concerned not only with criminal justice as such but with the basic principles of the maintenance of law and order, a recommendation which deserves to be taken into account, and which up to now has not received much attention from many governments which interpret 'law and order' in a very narrow sense. Experience shows that in far too many cases 'law and order' is interpreted as greater criminalization (involving some-times unjust treatment of ethnic groups), more severe penalties and extensive police powers.

The conclusion on the role of the community clearly shows the difficulties involved in its participation in the criminal justice system. The problem is in fact closely related to the type of society being evolved and the existing political regime which much too often does not comply with the purposes and principles of the Charter. Concerning the Standard Minimum Rules, the data submitted showed that only a small number of countries were applying them satisfactorily. Accordingly, and correctly, the vast majority of participants expressed the view that it was more important to ensure their more effective application than to revise the 1955 text.

The discussion on scientific approaches and research was interesting, and showed the futility of undertaking research into the causes of crime, an aim that fortunately was only supported by a small group of speakers. The consensus was that the primary object of research was not the identification of causes, but of factors that can be used for planned action. The conclusion was correct and it would deserve greater praise if, among the factors considered, the political had received attention.

The Fifth Congress was held in Geneva in 1975 under the slogan 'Crime Prevention and Control: the Challenge of the last Quarter of the Century'. The items on the agenda were: changes in forms and dimensions of criminality, transnational and national; criminal legislation, judicial procedures and other forms of control in the prevention of crime; the emerging role of the police and other law-enforcement agencies with special reference to changing expectations and minimum standards of performance; the treatment of offenders in custody or in the community, with special reference to the implementation of the Standard Minimum Rules; and economic and social consequences of crime and new challenges for research and planning.

In all 906 persons participated; 101 countries were represented by 549 delegates, 32 NGOs attended and there were 240 individual participants making up 26 per cent of the total. The specialized agencies already mentioned as well as Interpol and the IPPC were present, together with the Organization for Economic Cooperation and Development (OECD) and representatives of the Palestine Liberation Organization (PLO), the African National Congress of South Africa (ANC), and the Seychelles People's United Party.

The Fifth Congress made a series of recommendations of particular importance, many of them calling for action or to be brought to the attention of the different policy-making bodies, agencies and the CCPC. The recommendations were presented in a systematic way in the Report of the Congress, and for this the Secretariat should be congratulated again. The most salient matters were the adoption of a Declaration on the Protection of All Persons from Being Subjected to Torture and Other Cruel, Inhuman or Degrading Treatment or Punishment, subsequently adopted by General Assembly resolution 3452(XXX) December 1975 and the drafting of an international code of police ethics.

In addition the following matters were discussed: violence of transnational and comparative international significance; crime as business, organized crime, corruption and criminality; and drug abuse and alcoholism, among others. The following conclusions were adopted: social justice is the best means of preventing crime and greater emphasis should be placed on social action than on criminal proceedings; criminal policy should be coordinated and the whole integrated into the general social policy of the country; and victim compensation schemes could serve as useful substitutes for retributive criminal justice. The importance attached to human rights when discussing criminal justice matters was also one of the main characteristics of the Congress which, here again, deserves full praise.

The Sixth Congress was held in Caracas in 1980 and was attended by the representatives of 102 countries and the PLO, SWAPO, the ANC, the Pan Africanist Congress of Azania, ILO and WHO, the Council of Europe, Interpol, the League of Arab States, the Organization for African Unity (OAU), Organization of American States (OAS), the Pan-Arab Organization for Social Defence, 31 NGOs and about 220 individual participants plus 30 UN consultants. For economy reasons the report of the Congress does not contain enough data to determine the total number of participants but altogether there were probably almost 900.

The items on the agenda were: crime trends and crime prevention strategies; juvenile justice before and after the onset of delinquency; crime and the abuse of power; offences and offenders beyond the reach of the law; deinstitutionalization of correction and its implications for those remaining in prison; UN norms and guidelines in criminal justice from standard setting to implementation; capital punishment; new perspectives in crime prevention and criminal justice and development; the role of international cooperation.

The Congress adopted the Caracas Declaration, 19 resolutions and five decisions altogether involving more than a hundred requests for action from the UN, governments and international organizations. The main subjects covered were the promotion of broader public participation in crime prevention; the improvement of criminal statistics; the need for wide dissemination of knowledge of the nature and causes of crime as well as of measures ensuring its prevention; that the CCPC should be requested to develop standard minimum rules for the administration of juvenile justice; that the Secretary-General should assign to one of the UN prevention centres the responsibility for conducting research on the causes of juvenile delinquency; that extra-legal executions constitute a particularly abhorrent crime the eradication of which is a high international priority; that governments should take effective measures to prevent torture and related practices; that cooperative efforts should be intensified by member states to prevent, prosecute and control abuses of economic and political power that extend beyond national boundaries and territorial jurisdictions; that the CCPC should consider the question of alternatives to imprisonment; that prison systems should be sufficiently differentiated so as to allow the assignment of inmates in accordance with their needs in order to facilitate their placement in open institutions; that the CCPC should consider the question of measures for the social resettlement of prisoners; and the expression of a hope that the General Assembly would adopt the draft of Principles for the Protection of All Persons under the Declaration against Torture which was thoroughly discussed on the basis of a text submitted for that purpose at the 1975 Congress. The Caracas Declaration was presented at one of the last plenary meetings of the Congress, and adopted *nem. con.*

The provisional agenda adopted for the forthcoming Seventh Congress in Milan is as follows: new dimensions of criminality and crime prevention in the context of development; criminal justice processes and perspectives in a changing world; victims of crime; youth, crime and justice; and the formulation and application of UN standards and norms in criminal justice. With the exception of victims of crime, all other items should have been reduced to two, one on crime prevention in the context of development, and the other on the NINCJO. The reference to perspectives in a changing world is superfluous.

Whatever their shortcomings, the congresses remain one of the pillars of UN leadership in the field of criminal policy, particularly those of 1955, 1960, 1970 and 1975. The fact that many governments are remiss in implementing some of the fundamental recommendations does not alter this. Often the non-implementation is explained by saying that some of the recommendations run against national characteristics or tradition, that funds are not available, that recommendations are too numerous and sometimes contradictory, or that crime is not a serious problem in the non-implementing country. It would be difficult to maintain that any recommendation runs against national characteristics unless the objectors mean political persecution, apartheid and the like. Some recommendations may appear, prima facie, as not consonant with traditions, but in criminal policy matters old traditions are fading rapidly under the impact of post-industrial society, an impact which is far greater than that of industrial society. In any case congress recommendations, with some exceptions affecting the preservation of human rights, do not demand immediate but gradual implementation. Unfortunately some fundamental recommendations are still ignored after more than 25 years. The lack of financial resources cannot be denied but quite often the scarcity is due to the expenses involved in maintaining a dictatorial regime or in armament acquisitions. It cannot be denied that recommendations are too numerous and their proliferation should be avoided by formulating compact, clear recommendations instead of going into details or aspects which are part of a substantive recommendation. Occasionally recommendations contradict each other and the resulting confusion should be avoided by the congress, with the help of the Secretariat or the consultants appointed by it. Unfortunately such a task, which is not easy, can seldom be undertaken by the delegates, who are not always acquainted with UN criminal policies, but the same cannot be said about the Secretariat and the consultants who are supposed to be familiar with previous recommendations. The assertion that in some countries crime is not a problem is seldom convincing if account is taken of crimes resulting from the abuse of power. The adoption of the recommendations may have a preventive effect, and moreover by accepting them international cooperation will be reinforced.

It has also been said that congresses are becoming too expensive, the last time when the *Statement Submitted by the Secretary-General on the Budget Implications of the Preparations of the Seventh Congress on the Prevention of Crime and the Treatment of Offenders* (E/1982/ 37,Add.1,April 1982) was discussed at ECOSOC. Certainly some of the budgetary items are financially as well as politically objectionable. In all fairness it should be added that not all have been suggested by the Secretariat. The items concerning the travel and subsistence expenses for the participation of 'least developed' countries, the holding of five regional meetings and the participation of the regional commissions raise too many questions to be examined here. Suffice it to say that it would be extremely difficult to determine which are the 'least developed countries' as far as congresses are concerned: are they countries with a very low per capita income but with high internal expenses to maintain a dictatorial or authoritarian regime under which the criminal violation of human rights is more the rule than the exception? The proposal, which was not made by the Secretary-General, opens a new door to political manoeuvering already far too frequent among some groups of member states. The organization of regional preparatory meetings is being combined with the direct cooperation of the regional commissions, the UN Institutes and the governments which are supposed to help them. As for the appointment of consultants to the congress (there were no less than 30 at Caracas) it would be convenient to reduce their number if effective results are expected. The attendance of members of the CCPC, which is fully justified, has also been combined with the presence of 'least developed' countries, since many of them come from these countries and the same may be said about the regional preparatory meetings.

Analysis of the functioning of the congresses – the author was responsible for the organization of the first two as Chief of the Section of Social Defence, and has participated actively in the other four as head of delegation or as UN consultant – shows that gradually they are coming under excessive governmental control. In the last ten years the rules of procedure have been modified more than once so as to reduce individual and NGO participation to a minimum. At the early congresses the participation of these individuals or groups was extremely useful, and is in accordance with the purposes of UN criminal policy which do not confine themselves to the interests and aims of governments. It suffices to look at the summary records of the first two congresses to see that individual and NGO participation was justified, and the same may be said with respect to the 1970 and 1975 congresses. It may be argued that since governments are supposedly in charge of the implementation of the recommendations, their predominance at the congresses is justified. Apart from the fact that the implementation record of many of them is not what it should be, for many years it has been recommended that the community should actively participate in the prevention of crime, criminal justice and the treatment of offenders, and that community is essentially constituted by individuals, groups and organizations, so it is obvious that their growing participation in the discussions of the congresses is required. Why then their gradual exclusion? The answer probably lies in the fact that since most governments are dictatorial they are afraid that congresses may be used to criticize their often repressive criminal policies and programmes. Criticism may be well founded in some cases, particularly when it concerns a criminal abuse of power.[8]

Institutes
Logically, as part of the general centralized organization of the Secretariat at the beginning, the prevention of crime and the treatment of offenders were centred almost exclusively around the Section of Social Defence. But already by the 1950s and again as part of a general trend aiming at combining centralization with regionalization, it was clear that social defence activities should be partly regionalized in order to be more realistic and effective. In fact ECOSOC resolution 155 C(VII) 1948 was implicitly based on an overall consideration of the problem of crime which implied a close cooperation of the different regions of the world. UN leadership in criminal policy was never understood as aiming at uniformity, and still less at a governmental monopoly of the prevention of crime and the treatment of offenders. Accordingly, when the regional seminars for the preparation of the 1955 Congress were organized, as representative of the Secretary-General I suggested at the Latin American seminar, held in Rio de Janeiro and São Paulo in 1953, the organization of a UN Latin American institute the main purposes of which would be to carry out training courses and research, to assist the governments of the region; to provide advisory opinions in criminal

policy matters; to organize regional seminars; and to cooperate closely with the UN. The suggestion was accepted, and the seminar unanimously adopted a recommendation asking the UN to help in setting up the institute. I repeated it at the Asia and Far East seminar in Rangoon in 1954, with similar results. Almost simultaneously the suggestion was made by Paul Amor, senior member of the Section of Social Defence at the Arab seminar, in Cairo in 1953.

At present there are three UN institutes and the organization of a fourth (for Africa south of the Sahara) has been suggested on several occasions, most recently at the Caracas Congress and the latest session of the CCPC. It was also recommended by the Council of Ministers of the Organization of African Unity in 1979.

The UN Asia and Far East Institute (formerly UNAFEI, now AFEI), in the organization of which I had the privilege of participating actively with the Japanese authorities, is located at Fuchu, Tokyo, and was opened in 1962. Japan has acted as a generous host not only for the benefit of the countries of the region but also to some from other continents. Up to now, nearly 60 training courses have been organized, with a total attendance of nearly 2000 officials and professionals from more than 40 countries. The Institute regularly publishes a newsletter with the summaries of the training courses, and a bulletin called *Resource Material Series* with contributions and data on the prevention of crime, criminal justice, treatment and related subjects. In all the training courses the protection of human rights is emphasized, which is a splendid example. Participation in the training courses is characterized by discussions, evaluations and suggestions made by the participants. For the first ten years the UN provided the director, senior staff and financial assistance. In 1970 the responsibility passed to the government of Japan which continues to maintain the high reputation of the Institute, and also provides residential accommodation for students and visiting lecturers. This facility was agreed upon when the organization of UNAFEI was discussed.

While training, information, documentation and other activities are continuously expanding, research has been confined to more modest limits partly due to the fact that little can be done unless the governments of the region provide the required foundations for it. Australia is one of the exceptions and it is hoped that little by little the regional research situation may be improved under the Institute's guidance.[9]

The Latin American Institute (ILANUD) was established in 1975 at San José, Costa Rica, and since then the Costa Rican government has generously acted as host. As with UNAFEI, the UN helped during the first years financially and by providing senior staff and

professional assistance. ILANUD has organized a significant number
of training courses; convened regional as well as some international
meetings; acted as a clearing house; and rendered advisory services
to some of the governments of the region. It publishes periodically
a review, *ILANUD,* in which articles, studies, information, comments and a bibliography are made accessible to policy-makers and
professionals of the Latin American and Caribbean regions. Seminars
and symposia on criminal justice matters, correctional systems, mar-
ginality and delinquency, etc., have been organized, and the international meeting in 1978, at which the criminal abuse of power
was discussed, may be regarded as one of the most salient contributions to the study of the problem. The most commendable publications are *Manual de estadísticas criminales* (1982) and *El preso sin
condena en América Latina y el Caribe* (1983), both painstakingly
researched. It is hoped that the countries of the region will avail
themselves of the *Manual* in order to remedy the very unsatisfactory
condition of criminal statistics prevailing in most of them. As for
the unsentenced prisoner, *El preso sin condena* shows the need for
an urgent remedy. The data were provided by 30 countries, among
which Cuba does not appear, and show that the average in 18 countries is 69 per cent of the whole prison population. Three, Bolivia,
El Salvador and Paraguay have an average of 80 per cent and the
latter had 94.25 per cent in 1981.

Under an agreement between the UN and Egypt in 1972 a UN-
affiliated Institute of Social Defence, operating within the already
existing National Centre for Social and Criminological Research,
was created. The agreement lapsed in 1982.

For many years the Arab League has had its own Social Defence
Unit, and has frequently attended UN meetings, particularly those
of the CCPC. At its Ninth Arab Conference a Final Report, July
1978, was adopted as a contribution to the preparation for the 1980
UN Congress in which some principles and conclusions may be
found – such as that national security is closely related to internal
security, the breach of which is a breach of the necessary stability
for the military, political and economic power; crime prevention
and socioeconomic development should merge; crime prevention and
the protection of human rights are linked; and crime prevention
should be related to the cultural, social and demographic realities
of the Arab world.

In 1976 a symposium organized by the Kingdom of Saudi Arabia
on the effect of Islamic legislation on crime prevention in Saudi
Arabia was attended by several Arab countries and representatives
of the UN, ILANUD and the United Nations Social Defence Research Institute (UNSDRI). The Final Report is interesting since,

as in other regions of the world, it shows the differences among countries as far as crime is concerned, and therefore the difficulties involved in conducting research about its causes should be taken into account before undertaking any etiological research at the international level.[10]

In 1981 an agreement was signed between the UN and Finland by which the Helsinki Institute for Crime Prevention and Control, or HEUNI affiliated to the UN, was created. Its main purpose is the promotion of European cooperation in crime prevention and control. The annual report for 1982 describes as its main functions the organization of seminars for policy-makers, administrators, etc., and the collection of data and research. Two studies have been undertaken, one on prosecutorial decision and the other on solitary confinement.

When the attempt made to pass UN social defence activities to an international organization failed in 1964, there arose from the ashes the idea of organizing a UN social defence research institute.[11] The suggestion was objected to by some European and still more by some non-European countries. The main objections were that it was unnecessary because there were regional institutes; that the location of the institute in Europe would make it more difficult to get support from European countries as the Council of Europe was supposed to take care of European criminal policy; that the location in Europe would not facilitate the use of the Institute by developing countries; and finally, that it would raise unnecessary difficulties in the coordination of its activities with those of the regional institutes. The UN Social Defence Research Institute (UNSDRI) was established in accordance with ECOSOC resolution 1086B,1965, and the agreement with the Italian government, which offered to act as host, was concluded in 1968. Since then, mostly owing to Italian generosity, UNSDRI has conducted very valuable studies and research in different countries on juvenile delinquency, correction, national crime and criminal justice statistics, social defence needs in developing countries, social maladjustment, criminal justice and human rights, public participation in crime prevention, economic crime, delay in the administration of justice, etc. A series of publications has been issued, one of which, *A World Directory of Criminological Institutes* (second edition, 1978), is extremely useful.

In spite of the constant support of the Italian government, UNSDRI has always suffered from lack of funds and like the regional institutes, deserves far more help than it receives. The sensible thing to do would be to transform UNSDRI into a training institute for policy-makers, highly placed officials and members of the judiciary in the formulation and implementation of criminal policy.

Specialized Agencies and International Organizations

From the outset the UN tried to ensure the cooperation of the specialized agencies and the discussions about how to do this started as early as 1946 at the Second and Third Committees of the General Assembly which prepared the corresponding agreements and the bases for future coordination between the specialized agencies and ECOSOC.

Concerning criminal policy matters the cooperation of the International Labour Office (ILO) started in 1954 at the European Consultative Group when the question of prison labour, as one of the items on the agenda of the First Congress, was discussed. At the Congress itself the representative of the ILO participated actively particularly when the question of the steps to be taken to review the Convention on Forced or Compulsory Labour was raised. At the same Congress the ILO submitted a report on juvenile delinquency viewed as a labour problem (ILO.D.E.55). Since then the ILO has attended all congresses and cooperated with the UN. At the Second Congress in 1960, it submitted a report, *Treatment of Prisoners and After-care (Vocational Guidance, Training and Placement)* (A/CONF.17/13), and at the Third, in connection with juvenile delinquency, it submitted a paper dealing with employment opportunity and work in youth adjustment (A/CONF.26/L.1).

UNESCO has also regularly attended the UN congresses and submitted papers on some of the items, particularly at the Second and Third Congresses in connection with juvenile delinquency and the role of youth centres and schools. Some of its publications should be regarded as a form of cooperation in the study of problems dealt with by UN criminal policy. Such is the case with the volume *La violence et ses causes,* (Paris, 1980), in which the role of mass communications, criminological aspects of violence, violence and social defence, violence and repression and silent violence should be taken into account by policies and programmes against violent forms of crime.

The cooperation of World Health Organization (WHO) has been particularly frequent and valuable not only at the congresses and regional meetings but also in the research conducted on some subjects and publications. For the list of its contributions to the congresses, the corresponding reports should be consulted. The contributions deal with the prevention of juvenile delinquency, the causes and prevention of crime, alcohol and crime, abnormal offenders, criminal statistics and psychosocial indexes, deprivation of maternal care, delinquency in Africa, health and social defence planning, and juvenile justice systems. Of particular significance was the contribution of WHO in the discussion of abnormal offenders at the European

Consultative Group in 1956, which remains as valid today as it was then.[12] No less significant is the paper submitted at the Fifth Congress 1975, *Health Aspects of Avoidable Maltreatment of Prisoners and Detainees* (A/CONF.56/9), on health ethics, evolving attitudes to the treatment of offenders, forms of maltreatment, drug-dependent persons, forcible feeding, punishment for disciplinary offences, methods of restraint and intensive interrogation techniques unfortunately not always taken into account by specialists at the national level.[13]

The study of the relationship between narcotics and crime has been greatly facilitated by the work done by the International Narcotics Control Board, the United Nations Fund for Drug Abuse and Control and the Commission on Narcotic Drugs. The legal bases for their activities are the 1961 Single Convention and the Convention on Psychotropic Substances of 1971. In carrying out its work the Commission on Narcotic Drugs has also taken into account the contributions made on medical, educational and work aspects by WHO, UNESCO and ILO, which have contributed to the acceptance of the perception of the drug abuser as a person who should be given medical treatment and the view that the abuse of drugs is primarily a social problem.[14] As a sequel to this approach ECOSOC adopted two resolutions, both in 1975, one (resolution 1934(LVIII)) recommending governments to incorporate the necessary measures for the treatment of drug abusers into their public health programmes; and the other (resolution 1932(LVIII)) inviting them to take into consideration the pertinent recommendations and resolutions adopted by the organs of the UN as well as by other international bodies for the suppression of illicit traffic in narcotic drugs and psychotropic substances. In view of the increasing gravity of the financial aspect of the illicit traffic, in 1975 ECOSOC adopted resolution 2002(LX) urging governments which had not already done so to enact the necessary legislation so as to make it a punishable offence knowingly to provide financial support in furtherance of the offences enumerated in the Single Convention. In some countries the financial value of illicit traffic is one of the biggest items of national income.

The United Nations Fund for Drug Abuse Control acts as a sort of clearing house, and as a link between organizations executing projects and donor countries. These functions are conducted at the regional and country level. The projects include assistance to governments in enacting and revising legislation; assistance to farmers in the replacement of narcotic crops; information programmes; research; and the repression of illicit traffic.[15]

Analysis of the *Review of the Illicit Traffic in Narcotic Drugs and Psychotropic Substances during 1979* (E/CN/7/666), the *Report of the*

Commission on Narcotic Drugs, 29th Session (E/1981/24) and of the *Study on Measures to Reduce Illicit Demand for Drugs* (United Nations 1979), shows that information, education and treatment play a role in the prevention of drug addiction but that their role is very limited as far as the reduction of illicit traffic is concerned. The main reason is that although strategies, evolving patterns, measurement issues, rehabilitation, the goal of prevention, confidentiality and many other subjects deserve expert attention, far more should be given to corruption, venality and gross negligence as conditioning factors not only of illicit traffic but also of drug abuse. But they are seldom referred to in the discussions and reports based on the answers received from governments. While in the *Survey of National Programmes Aimed at Reducing Illicit Demand for Drugs,* which is part of the *Study on Measures to Reduce Illicit Demands for Drugs,* I found numerous references to information, educational and other programmes, I failed to find any concerning the prevention of the three conditioning factors mentioned above. The analysis of the data on the 85 countries included shows that in quite a number of them the programmes described coexist with an almost blatant non-implementation of the conventions and of the national legislation on narcotic drugs.

As the *Study* states, it is true that in some cases legislation may be a stimulus for greater demand, but the stimulus would be considerably reduced if it were not so excessively repressive and the legislation was implemented. A review of the countries which are parties to the conventions shows that in some of them the impact of corruption, venality and negligence is powerful enough to obliterate the little that is done at the national level as far as information, education and treatment is concerned.

Illicit traffic, demand for drugs and drug addiction are closely related to crime although the relationship is not the same in each of the three aspects mentioned. Of the three, the first benefits from impunity, particularly when carried out in an organized way. Its reduction is prevented by corruption, venality and gross negligence at the high political and administrative levels to which all other levels are subordinated, particularly when the country is under a dictatorial regime. Here again the collusion between the abuse of power and crime is obvious. It is significant that the victimization of almost all other countries may be regarded as the 'work' of a few developing ones. It may be argued that organized illicit traffic has other roots, but whatever they are the fact remains that the bulk of the raw material used is provided by a handful of developing countries. Would their role be prevented with better socioeconomic development? Would the existence of a new international economic order help? Would a public and objective exposé of that 'work' at the international level contribute to a reduction of illicit production and traffic? Would economic sanctions reduce both? Suffice it to say that the present low-level approach to illicit production and traffic pays dividends mostly only to the traffickers and those serving them at every level, and that since international and national machinery are interdependent the reasonable functioning of the first cannot take place when the second is out of order.   At its January 1985 session the International Narcotics Control Board stressed the increasing gravity of the illicit traffic in drugs which leads to greater consumption and which in some countries is facilitated by permissive legislation concerning the possession of drugs for personal consumption. It was pointed out that Peru and Bolivia should take the necessary steps to reduce the growing and uncontrolled cultivation of coca leaves which, incidentally, was recommended by the UN Commission of Inquiry in 1949. According to the report, with the exception of Eastern Europe all other countries are affected by the increase in the illicit consumption of drugs.

The International Criminal Police Commission, Interpol, has constantly cooperated with the UN in criminal policy matters. It suffices to review the reports of the Congresses to see that Interpol has contributed to practically all of them by submitting reports or by participating actively in the discussions. Of particular significance were the papers submitted on *Special Police Departments for the Prevention of Juvenile Delinquency* (1960), *The Role and Future of the Police in the Field of Crime Prevention* (1965), and *The Role the Police in Terms of Their Prevention and Social Activities,* (1975). During the discussion of the emerging role of the police and other law enforcement agencies at the Fifth Congress the interventions made by Interpol were constructive and to the point. One of them referred to the limited practicability of training policemen at an international academy, which would tend to confine itself to a few specialized subjects by reason of the national diversity in legal and police systems; another comment was that Interpol has no supranational police power, which is particularly important when analysing the data sent to it by the national police forces and the role played by them under dictatorial regimes.

The International Civil Aviation Organization (ICAO) has played an important role since the 1950s in the prevention of crime at the international level, particularly concerning hijacking and related criminal offences. As a result of its endeavours the International Conference on Air Law, held in Tokyo in 1963, led to the Convention on Offences and Certain Other Acts Committed On Board Aircraft, which came into force in 1969. It applies to acts against penal law and to those which, whether or not they constitute offences, may or do jeopardize the safety of the aircraft or of the persons or property therein or which jeopardize good order and discipline on board. In 1970 the Convention for the Suppression of Unlawful Seizure of Aircraft was signed at The Hague, and came into effect in 1971. This applies to offences or attempted offences committed by force or threat or by any other form of intimidation. It was promptly realized that the Hague Convention should be supplemented by a third one, and to that effect an international conference was convened in Montreal in 1971 and the Convention for the Suppression of Unlawful Acts against the Safety of Civil Aviation adopted; it came into force in 1973. The offences covered are any act of violence committed against a person on board an aircraft in service or the destruction and damage caused to air navigation facilities if any of such acts is likely to endanger the safety of aircraft in flight. Annex 17 to the Convention, applicable since 1975, aims at safeguarding international civil aviation against acts of unlawful interference, and deals primarily with organizational and administrative matters which are relevant to crime prevention.[16]

Here again the effectiveness of the conventions and corresponding machinery may be seriously affected by the behaviour of governments which, for political reasons, do not become parties to the conventions, or, if they do, do not always act in accordance with their provisions. Do international conventions deter individuals, organizations or governments sufficiently to justify the efforts made to draft them and to get them into force? Would it not be better to consider such offences for what they are – common offences committed in a particular place, which does not change the character of the offence and should be subject to extradition whatever the ideological aims of the offender? This raises the question of the specificity of the political offence, which will be discussed when dealing with terrorism.

Recently the enormous number of refugees in Africa, Asia, the Caribbean and Latin America has raised the question of whether the frequent crimes committed against and among them make more difficult the prevention of crime and the treatment of the offenders involved. Are the 1951 Convention and the 1967 Protocol relating to the status of refugees and the UN Declaration on Territorial Asylum of 1967 really applied? A study of the *Conclusions on the Protection of Refugees adopted by the Executive Committee of the United Nations High Commissioner for Refugees* (Geneva 1980), based on the three instruments mentioned, shows that here again individuals as well as organizations and governments are involved in the perpetration of a great number of criminal offences, partly due to the non-implementation of these instruments.

Although there have always been refugees, it was the proliferation of dictatorial regimes in the second part of the twentieth century which rapidly increased their number, as well as increasing the inhuman, cruel and degrading treatment meted out to them, in many cases as easy prey. Political persecution is one of the main conditioning factors, the effect of which is aggravated by political and racial incomprehension, leading to exploitation and frequent criminal violation of human rights. The crimes committed are often published by the press, seldom prosecuted, and rarely appear in criminal statistics. The offenders are government authorities mostly of coastal states, a new type of slave-trader, organized gangs and individuals. The offences most frequently involved are murder, bodily or mental injury, rape, exploitation, moral degradation and fraud. In spite of its extent and gravity this new kind of crime has received little attention in the formulation of national and international criminal policies and programmes.[17]

As a regional organization related to the UN, the Council of Europe should be considered here inasmuch as its criminal policy is often related to or considered as an extension of that of the UN.

In 1957 the Committee of Foreign Ministers set up the European Committee on Crime Problems, and gave it a mandate to implement a European policy in this field which, as has already been explained, eventually contributed to the fading out of the European Consultative Group and the United Nations Consultative Group. The Committee is composed of representatives from all member states of the Council. It is assisted by the Criminological Scientific Council and the Conference of Directors of Criminological Research Institutes, and at the Secretariat level by the Division of Crime Problems, which is part of the Directorate of Legal Affairs. Over nearly 25 years, the Committee has successfully undertaken a great variety of studies related to crime prevention, criminal justice and the treatment of offenders. It has also prepared several conventions and a large number of resolutions addressed to governments, and has sponsored an exchange of research workers and penitentiary staff. It publishes an international bulletin which is very informative.[18]

The most recent publications are *Report on the Standard Minimum Rules for the Treatment of Prisoners* (1980); *Compensation of Victims of Crime* (1978); *The Contribution of Criminal Law to the Protection of Environment* (1980); *Criminological Aspects of the Ill-treatment of Children in the Family* (1981); *Prevention of Juvenile Delinquency* (1981); and *International Exchange of Information on Current Criminological Projects in Member States* (1982). Up to June 1981 there were 50 resolutions on crime problems. It is significant that

one of the current projects, to be completed in 1985, is to review
the operation of 14 conventions in which penal and related matters
are dealt with. In sum, the Council of Europe makes a leading
contribution to the formulation of international criminal policy.

With respect to the other regional organizations, very little can
be said as far as criminal policy is concerned. Putting aside some
peripheral activities in juvenile delinquency matters, the most significant and recent contribution of the Organization of American States
was the *Informe sobre la situación de los derechos humanos en Argentina*
(Washington, 1980), for which the OAS deserves congratulations.
The report, which deals among other important matters with the
rights to life, freedom, justice and other fundamental human rights,
examines the question of missing persons. Its content confirms again,
in a different setting, that whatever the country or region contemplated crime cannot be confined, as still pretended by some, to common crime. It was the conservative criminology of the nineteenth
century which imposed scientifically such a narrow conception of
crime, and with it a useless 'prevention of crime' and the fiction,
professionally cultivated in developed countries, of the rehabilitation
of the offender who, as a rule, was a member of the less privilieged
social classes.

The Secretariat
Although the last to be dealt with, the Secretariat is by no means
the least in the machinery of the UN. Operationally, in fact, it is
the mainspring, without which it would be difficult to envisage the
functioning of the other principal bodies. By 'operational' is understood not only the Secretariat's professional-administrative capacity
in organizing the UN by servicing its main bodies and subsidiaries,
but also its role in assisting such bodies in the fulfilment of their
functions and when necessary making use of its own right to initiate.
The Secretary-General personifies all these and related activities
which in most cases, particularly concerning criminal policy matters,
are performed by members of the Secretariat representing him on
the different councils, commissions, committees, groups of experts
and other meetings. Internally, the operational activities are led by
the heads of departments, centres, divisions, branches, sections, etc.
All this means that the Secretariat is expected to provide the policy-
making bodies and subsidiaries with the information and data
required on matters under consideration. In spite of its knowledge
and efforts this is not always possible, particularly when the information sought is supposed to be provided by governments. Quite
often, for reasons which are not always in agreement with UN pur-

poses and principles, the information or data are not provided by the member states.

Being an organization, the UN is a system constituted by six subsystems which are the principal bodies enumerated in article 7 of the Charter, one of which is the Secretariat. Putting aside the International Court of Justice which in some cases may play a role in UN criminal policy, the other bodies deal with such policy in different contexts. The fact that crime is dealt with in different contexts does not mean that the various aspects of it are not parts of the same whole. War crimes or crimes against mankind are in fact common crimes committed with more powerful means than common crimes but sometimes with the same aims.

The Secretariat is a policy-making body not only because of its advisory and consultative functions, which in certain cases may carry great weight in taking a decision, but also in its own right, particularly when a question requires an immediate decision or when the recommendation adopted by another policy-making body gives the Secretariat latitude to act on its own initiative. This policy-making function is not always well known and is sometimes resented, particularly in criminal policy matters where too often criminal violation of human rights, summary executions, crimes against mankind, etc., are involved. As we will see, the problem of crime is being more affected than ever by sociopolitical questions in which ideology, sovereignty, state or government prerogatives and power play a role. In this respect it should be borne in mind that many of the regimes of the member states are dictatorial. Such predominance of dictatorial regimes does not facilitate the task of the Secretariat in criminal policy matters, hence the open or veiled hostility to UN criminal policy of some regimes.

In carrying out UN criminal policy the Secretariat is often confronted with a multiplicity of difficulties which for our purposes may be grouped as follows: firstly, the relatively binding character of the resolutions of the policy-making bodies; secondly, lack of cooperation; and thirdly, the scarcity of ways and means.

Binding character of resolutions
In principle all resolutions have a binding character, the extent of which may vary according to what has been decided upon. It is expected that resolutions will be adopted in accordance with the purposes and principles of the UN. Unfortunately, confining ourselves to UN leadership in criminal policy, this is not always the case, which means that in order to solve the contradiction, the Secretariat has to take its own decision in conformity with the purposes and principles mentioned.

The cases of contradiction, without being too numerous, are important enough to deserve a few comments. One of the most flagrant is General Assembly resolution 32/60, 3 January 1978, which, after stating in its first paragraph 'that crime in its various forms hampers the economic, social and cultural development of peoples and threatens the enjoyment of human rights and fundamental freedoms', nevertheless reaffirms 'the right of each State to formulate and implement its national policies and programmes in the field of crime prevention and control in accordance with its own needs and priorities'. Putting aside the fact that the first paragraph does not mention political development (which should not be identified with, although closely related to, human rights and fundamental freedoms), the contradiction between the two paragraphs is obvious, and scarcely veils the resistance to UN criminal policy of some governments. The world panorama of crime clearly shows that a large amount of contemporary crime is due to the criminal abuse of power by states particularly keen on satisfying their needs and priorities. Otherwise it would be difficult to explain the growing extent of genocide, torture, cruel, inhuman or degrading treatment, missing persons, summary or arbitrary executions, and so on.

Certainly the needs and priorities of the state should be taken into account, provided that their satisfaction is not against the UN purposes and principles and the corresponding UN criminal policy. It may be argued that, since the relevant phrases are in the descriptive and not in the operative part of the resolution, the criticism made here is unfounded. In rebuttal it should be pointed out that the descriptive clauses refer to what are considered the foundations of the resolution; the resolution tries to assert an identification between peoples and states which, besides being sociopolitically and juridically incorrect, is against the purposes and principles of the Charter which was actually promulgated by the peoples of the United Nations.

The matter is extremely important if it is remembered that in some cases the Secretariat may refrain from taking a particular line of action in criminal policy in the mistaken belief that the states and not the peoples are the constituents of the UN. Fortunately, the Secretariat has always loyally adhered to the purposes and principles of the Charter by bringing into UN criminal policy matters such as, for example, the criminal abuse of power which, as we will see, shows how often peoples are the victims of such abuse.

Sometimes the Secretariat may be tempted to follow theories or criminal policies prevailing in certain countries regarded as criminologically progressive and bring them into UN programmes. The temptation should be avoided by keeping in mind that UN leadership in criminal policy must be based on the heterogeneous needs and priorities of a variety of peoples and not on models offered here and there which have often failed in the very countries in which they were produced.

Cooperation

At the international level cooperation between governments and the UN and within the Secretariat is far from what it should be. Suffice it to say here that the implementation of a number of General Assembly and ECOSOC resolutions is much too often less than satisfactory. The limited effectiveness in many countries of the Standard Minimum Rules for the Treatment of Prisoners, 25 years after being adopted by ECOSOC, is significant. The adoption in 1975 of the Declaration Against Torture and Cruel, Inhuman and Degrading Treatment or Punishment has not prevented the regimes pactising them from continuing their criminal behaviour. The limited number of answers from governments to questionnaires sent to them by the Secretariat on behalf of the General Assembly and ECOSOC cannot always by explained by scarcity of ways and means or because the matter does not affect the governments.

Although the Crime Prevention and Criminal Justice Branch is primarily in charge of UN criminal policy, other services dealing with human rights, narcotics, population, social and economic development, statistics, legal questions, transnational corporations and other matters also deal with aspects of that policy. When it is remembered that this also happens with the Specialized Agencies, the question of ensuring cooperation and coordination in a more effective way is becoming a crucial matter if better results and a saving of effort and money are to be achieved.

for the Biennium 1982–1983, Vol. I, Supplement 6 (A/36/6,1981); *Proposed Medium-Term Plan for the Period 1984–1989* (A/37/6,1982); *Interagency Aspects of the Follow-up to the Sixth United Nations Congress on the Prevention of Crime and the Treatment of Offenders* (ACC.1981/PG/11,1981); *Resolutions and Decisions Adopted by the General Assembly during its Thirty-Sixth Session*, Supplement 51 (A/36/511,1982) and the last report of the CCPC (E/CN.5/1983) clearly shows:

(1) the growing complexity, gravity and extent of crime at the national and international levels, in all of which political regimes of many sorts, ideological organizations, transnational corporations and different types of institution and movement are deeply implicated;

(2) that criminal policy is dealt with by a plurality of Secretariat services, which confirms the complexity of crime as a growing international and transnational phenomenon – at the Thirty-Sixth Session of the General Assembly no less than 28 resolutions directly concerning crime problems were adopted;

(3) that with some exceptions, the most marked being the Divisions of Human Rights and Narcotic Drugs, the Secretariat services dealing with criminal policy do not cooperate as they should.

The coordinating functions of the Secretariat's criminal policy responsibilities should be in the hands of the Centre for Social and Humanitarian Affairs and the CCPC, and operated by the Branch. These activities do not mean interference in the programmes of other services but simply a greater sense of collective responsibilty in carrying out a policy which, owing to its multiple aspects, requires a cooperation which cannot be reduced to 'expressing interest' when approached by the Branch to work together on a particular aspect of criminal policy. Cooperation should also be sought from the United Nations Institute for Training and Research (UNITAR) which, up to now, has remained aloof from criminal policy matters. Research on the analysis of the existing resolutions and evaluating them would be a worthwhile project.

Availability of ways and means
The precarious financial condition of the UN, partly a result of the arrears in the payment of contributions by a sizeable number of governments, makes more difficult the devotion of more resources to carrying out criminal policy programmes. To this should be added the hostility of some governments to that policy. On the other hand, lack of finances can partly be compensated for by a more effective cooperation not only within but also outside the Secretariat, i.e. with the specialized agencies, regional commissions and the institutes.

The lack of resources is obvious in the work of the Branch, which in the past few years has been compelled to confine itself more and more to the preparation of Congresses which, although important, is not the primary responsibility of UN leadership. Yet in many subtle ways such 'confinement' is taking place in spite of the efforts of the Branch to liberate itself. Even concerning the congresses, a comparative study shows that while in the past they benefited from other activities of the Secretariat this is gradually fading. Even the contents of the reports are being reduced for economy reasons. The Caracas Congress report was not even printed like the previous ones, but merely mimeographed and its contents reduced to a minimum.

As for the personnel assigned to the Branch, although recently it has been increased, a comparison with that existing in the past and the corresponding tasks clearly shows that in spite of the devotion and efforts of the staff, it cannot carry out the existing programmes. Here again reference is made to the documents mentioned in the section on co-operation ((b) above). It should be added that if the coordinating functions were assigned to the Branch, a staff member would be required to deal with them.

The situation is well known in the upper echelons of the Secretariat, which are fully aware of the need for greater responsiveness to UN criminal policy. Criminal policy and development are closely related, but the solution does not lie in transforming that policy into an aspect of development, but in reaffirming the relationship and at the same time the substantivity of the crime problem. In other words, after evaluation of what is being done what is needed is to set up a Secretariat division capable not only of carrying out its own crime prevention and criminal justice programmes but of making effective the coordination of UN leadership in criminal policy. Such a move would be fully justified; it must be remembered that contrary to what is said even by General Assembly resolution 35/171, 5 February 1981, the responsibility of such leadership did not originate in General Assembly resolution 415(V), December 1950, transferring the functions of the IPPC to the UN. This mistake has its parallel in the assertion, sometimes made by the Secretariat itself, that the origin of the CCPC is that resolution. A careful reading of antecedents shows how erroneous that is.

In sum, as far as criminal policy and leadership are concerned, the Secretariat is confronted with increasing difficulties, many of which may be disposed of and others considerably reduced if, after an evaluation of what is being done in that field (not only by the Branch), the Branch could be provided with more adequate ways and means to fulfil its responsibilities. It should be kept in mind that contrary to some governmental assertions, crime is becoming less and less a domestic problem. Even common crime is acquiring an extent and gravity which goes beyond national boundaries. If as repeatedly stated 'the phenomenon of crime, through its impact on society, impairs the overall development of nations, undermines people's spiritual and material well-being, compromises human dignity and creates a climate of fear and violence that endangers personal security and erodes the quality of life', (see resolution 35/171 already mentioned) why not make an effort and provide the Secretariat, as the main operational body, with the resources required to prevent all that?

Notes

1. For a detailed consideration of its origin, evolution and present scope see M. López-Rey, *Crime, an Analytical Appraisal* (1970).

2. In 1977 the General Assembly requested the Commission on Human Rights to draw up a draft Convention on the subject in the light of the principles embodied in the Declaration which was finalized and adopted by the Commission in 1984.

3. For details of arrangements for NGOs with consultative status see ECOSOC resolution 288(X),1950.

4. At the Caracas Congress the subject was discussed but no recommendation was made. Action no. 2 refers only to capital punishment which was sent back to the 'legislative bodies' of the UN.

5. Originally the number of members of the ad hoc committee did not exceed seven but ECOSOC raised the number to ten in 1965, to 15 in 1971 and to 27 in 1979 as indicated.

6. For further details on the work done by the Committee see its Report (E/1980,112, October 1980).

7. At its 1981 session the Commission, after discussing the matter, decided that 'crime and criminal justice should continue to be considered in the context of social development and that, therefore, the Commission was the competent body to deal with the Committee's report' (E/CN.5/598,1981, p. 33). The fact that something may be considered in the context of something else does not mean that other contexts should be excluded. As we will see later, development means far more than social development, therefore, although competent in some respects, the Commission is not the only competent body and like the Human Rights and Narcotic Commissions the logical solution is that the Committee should report directly to ECOSOC. Actually a close reading of paragraph 88 of the Commission's report shows that the coordination problem raised by the Committee at its 1980 meeting had not been considered – perhaps for lack of time.

8. The reader is referred to the *International Review of Criminal Policy*, no. 27 (not recent, but still valid in many respects), which includes a series of interesting papers on public participation in criminal justice, use of volunteers, mobilization of public opinion, contribution of NGOs to the formulation of criminal policies and programmes, etc., by C.S. Versele, Y. Shiono, P. Könz, T.O. Elias, Milton G. Rector, Boris A. Victorov, H. Quijada and W.H. Wickwar. For other important NGO contributions see issue no. 35, in which the activities and co-

operation of the International Society of Social Defence, the Salvation Army, International Police Association, etc., are described. Of primary importance is the cooperation of Amnesty International and the International Commission of Jurists.

9. The Australian Institute of Criminology has contributed with the publication of *Innovations in Criminal Justice in Asia and the Pacific,* 1979, edited by W. Clifford assisted by S.D. Gokhale. It is significant that more than half the contributors have been associated in different ways with UNAFEI, among them V.N. Pillai, a former director. Clifford was for several years UN Senior Adviser.

10. The translation into French, English and Spanish of the *Proceedings* was undertaken by UNSDRI. The English translation was made available in 1980 by the Ministry of Interior, Crime Prevention Centre, Kingdom of Saudi Arabia.

11. See the first and second reports annexed to document E/CN.5/ 383.

12. *See United Nations European Consultative Group, Third Session* (Prison Printing Shops, Melun 1957), chapter II.

13. A comparison between the WHO paper and the *Summary of the Explanatory Memorandum on the Prison Law No.47,1395* (1975) submitted by the Libyan delegation to the same Congress would be extremely interesting.

14. By social should be understood sociopolitical, a characteristic which is ignored by those advocating the 'legalization' of at least certain drugs. The question was raised at the Fifth Congress when some aspects of decriminalization and depenalization were discussed. Fortunately the representative of the Narcotics Division reasserted the policy of the UN which is against the 'legalization' of the drugs covered by the Conventions. The sociopolitical character of the problem has been stressed by the writer in his paper 'Drug Addiction as a Sociopolitical Problem', *Journal of Drug Issues* (1974).

15. For some details of the machinery dealt with in this section see issue no. 34 of the *International Review of Criminal Policy.*

16. For more detailed information see K. Hammarskjöld, 'Air Piracy as an International Crime: Suggestions for International Action', *International Review of Criminal Policy,* no. 32, (1976).

17. For an account of the background and actual situation of the refugee problem, see S. Aga Khan, *Study on Human Rights and Massive Exodus* (E/CN.4/1503,1981) which is part of the more general question of the violation of human rights and fundamental freedom studied by the UN Division of Human Rights; and the *Summary Report with Conclusions and Recom-*

mendations (UNESCO, 1982) of the Symposium on the Promotion, Dissemination and Teaching of Fundamental Rights of Refugees, held in Tokyo in 1981.

18.   For more details see issue no. 34 of the *International Review of Criminal Policy*.

3 Main subjects of United Nations criminal policy

Following a broadly chronological order, the main subjects of UN criminal policy are:
(1) genocide;
(2) war crimes and crimes against peace and mankind;
(3) juvenile delinquency;
(4) Standard Minimum Rules for the Treatment of Prisoners;
(5) selection and training of personnel;
(6) open penal and correctional institutions;
(7) prison labour;
(8) medicopsychological and social examination of offenders;
(9) detention of adults prior to sentencing;
(10) criminal statistics;
(11) short-term imprisonment and alternatives to imprisonment;
(12) pre-release treatment and after-care;
(13) crime and development;
(14) capital punishment;
(15) police programmes, activities and functions;
(16) abnormal and habitual offenders;
(17) recidivism;
(18) community preventive action and participation in criminal justice;
(19) social change and social forces and the prevention of crime;
(20) specific preventive and treatment measures for young adults;
(21) the planning of criminal justice;
(22) research;
(23) change in forms and dimensions of criminality;
(24) economic consequences of crime;
(25) criminal law and criminal procedure matters;
(26) criminality related to motorized traffic;
(27) terrorism;
(28) torture and cruel, inhuman or degrading treatment or punishment;
(29) arbitrary executions and missing persons;
(30) illicit payments;
(31) criminal corruption;

(32) illicit production, traffic and use of drugs;

(33) extent and trends of crime;

(34) criminalization and decriminalization;

(35) norms and guidelines in criminal justice;

(36) crime and the abuse of power;

(37) criminal justice processes and perspectives in a changing world;

(38) formulation of a new international-national criminal justice order;

(39) victims of crime;

(40) youth, crime and justice;

(41) guiding principles for crime prevention and criminal justice.

The list would be longer if specific reference were made to topics which are aspects of larger ones. This is particularly the case with some items concerning treatment. Quite often the same subject has been discussed several times under different headings or as something related to a main item. Police matters have been examined on several occasions by referring to police activities, programmes or functions, and this culminated with the adoption by the General Assembly of the Code for Law Enforcement Officers in 1977. As we will see, juvenile delinquency has been repeatedly dealt with and the last discussion on the matter, at the Caracas Congress, implies a regression from, if not a negation of, much that had been stated before. The abuse of power embraces many forms, and consequently a variety of kinds of crime among which torture and cruel, inhuman or degrading treatment or punishment and economic crime are two of the most significant.

Analysis of the list of criminal policy topics shows:

(a) The importance attached from the beginning to crimes such as genocide and the criminal violation of human rights, which clearly demonstrates that, contrary to a widely accepted way of thinking, crime is essentially a single global phenomenon and that the separation between common and non-conventional offences is more apparent than real. It may be maintained that what are called special crimes are simply different types of the older common crimes in which modern ways and means are used for their perpetration. Another fundamental conclusion is that in many cases crime implies the flagrant violation of human rights individually or collectively understood.

(b) The evolution from a markedly treatment-oriented international criminal policy towards a wider one in which socioeconomic and political questions are involved is manifest. This reflects the appreciation, particularly by the Secretariat, of the gradual expansion of post-industrial society, in which decolonization has played a role, and the growing failure of national and international criminal policy attempts to deal with the various kinds of crime.

(c) The fragmentation of items is to a great extent due to the empirical approach to the problem still prevailing in many countries, often due to professional assertions always ready to emphasize the importance of a particular aspect without seeing that the best thing to do with it is to study it as part of the larger one to which it belongs. As we will see, the planning of criminal policy came rather late, and even now is still stubbornly refused by many countries more interested in introducing a multiplicity of penal reforms than in planning the penal systems which they need. Certainly in some cases fragmentation is needed, but as a rule it should be avoided when dealing with criminal justice matters.

In sum, the evolution towards a global conception of crime, in which national and international levels can hardly be separated, implies a criminal policy in which not only individuals but also institutions, parties, organizations, corporations and regimes act criminally.

Quite a number of subjects have been introduced by the Secretariat, particularly the Branch and the Division of Human Rights, which from the beginning have enjoyed a close mutual understanding and effective cooperation. One of the first initiatives of the Section of Social Defence was to restrict the meaning of juvenile delinquency; another to stress the connection of criminal policy with development. More recently the need for planning, the abuse of power and victimization have been brought in by a Branch alert to the transformation of crime and the need for penal systems very different from those in existence. Other subjects have been the result of Congress recommendations which, although valuable, tend sometimes to fragmentation or repetition. Less frequently a particular subject has been incorporated into UN criminal policy as the result of a recommendation by the General Assembly: such is the case, for example, with capital punishment. As for ECOSOC its role is also extremely significant as regards the preparation of Congresses, and also in the enlargement of the functions of the CCPC, which has led to its greater intervention in the formulation of programmes.

Occasionally a subject is dropped because substantively it has little or no justification, or because it has already been dealt with as part of a larger one. Among others, this was the case with the institutional treatment of women, jointly initiated more than thirty years ago by the Sections of Social Defence and Status of Women in compliance with ECOSOC resolution 204(XI), 1951. Governments were not very receptive to it and the data provided by them was scanty and mostly of limited value. It was correctly said that the treatment of women was part of general treatment, and the specificity of women's needs was to be covered by appropriate provisions of the Standard Minimum Rules which was drafted at that time – see rule 23. Yet under the impact of the women's movement, which indeed deserves praise, the matter was revived at the Caracas Congress which adopted a resolution asking, among other things, for continued efforts 'to ensure that the woman offender be treated fairly and equally under arrest, trial, sentence and imprisonment'. A first reading of what has been said and recommended on the matter of detention, arrest, etc., since 1950 in a diversity of meetings and documents in the UN will show that not only women but everyone is covered by the recommendations made.

Of greater significance and more in accordance with the equality of rights between men and women in contemporary post-industrial society, the Secretariat submitted to the CCPC at its 1984 session an interesting report, *Women and the Criminal Justice System* (E/AC. 57/1984/15), in which the responses of 46 governments through their national correspondents, supplemented by information provided by UNAFEI, ILANUD, UNSDRI and HEUNI were examined. Briefly, the findings are that the majority of women particularly in some developing countries, are still involved in supportive and clerical duties; that in some countries their appointment to high judicial and police posts is being encouraged and facilitated; and that more women should become educated in law and social sciences so that their qualifications enable them to compete with men for high positions in the criminal justice system.

As for women's treatment as offenders, the information provided shows that in some cases they are treated preferentially, while in others they are subject to harsher measures, particularly in some developing countries and mostly for moral and religious reasons. Since females constitute a proportionally smaller incarcerated population it is not feasible in many countries to employ special full-time treatment staff. But most countries report that special provisions are made to satisfy the needs of the pregnant prisoner and her offspring, an effort already required by the Standard Minimum Rules.

Since not all the subjects of UN criminal policy enumerated can be dealt with here, only a limited selection is examined.

Traffic in women
The traffic in women and children, prostitution and obscene publications was a subject inherited by the UN from the League of Nations.

In 1946–7 the Secretary-General was instructed to consider suitable measures for an effective campaign against such traffic, and for the suppression of prostitution and the circulation of obscene publications. Consequently, the effectiveness of the 1921 and 1923 Conventions on Traffic in Women and the 1923 Convention on Obscene Publications were studied as well as the draft of a new Convention.

In 1959 the study *Traffic in Persons and Prostitution*, based on the 1949 Convention, was published by the UN. It emphasizes that the prevention of prostitution depends on the programme of action in each country. As preventive measures it recommends the improvement of social and economic conditions, equal pay for men and women, educational training, sex and health education, improvement of the status of women and intensification of social services. In some respects the study anticipated much of what was later advocated under different policies and movements. Almost simultaneously, issue no. 13 of the *International Review of Criminal Policy* (1958) was devoted to the publication of several studies on prostitution and anti-venereal measures in ten selected countries. Although since then 25 years have elapsed, much of what was said then is still valid.

The list of *Human Rights International Instruments (Signatures, Ratifications, Accessions, etc., 1 July 1982)* (United Nations, 1982), which is not frequently used in criminal policy research, shows that up to now only 53 member states, or about 33 per cent of the total membership, are parties to the Convention for the Suppression of the Traffic in Persons and the Exploitation of the Prostitution of Others. In many cases that traffic and exploitation is a criminal offence, and is widespread in some countries, particularly those in which mass exodus of refugees takes place. Prostitution is still flourishing in many countries, developed or not, although the kind of development determines the kinds of prostitution and exploitation which are commercialized in some countries for the satisfaction of nationals or tourists or both. In some countries, prostitutes have organized themselves, pay taxes or try to pay them, and ask for professional recognition. In others, promiscuity has replaced prostitution, but still the exploitation of persons, particularly of children for prostitution purposes, is manifest. It should be noted that a large number of developing countries are not parties to the Convention, and it is here that the traditional factors conditioning prostitution and exploitation are still operating, sometimes on a large scale. A criminological comparison of these countries with the developing countries which are not parties to the Convention for the Protection of Refugees seems to confirm the relationship referred to above between prostitution, exploitation, refugee conditions and certain kinds of crime. In becoming parties to the Convention some of the socialist countries, when making their reservations, particularly to article 22 of the Convention concerning the jurisdiction of the International Court of Justice, stated that their socioeconomic conditions have eliminated those conditions leading to the commission of offences described by the Convention.

Concerning pornography it seems that some of the developed countries are the great producers. By acting in this way their role as leaders in other respects is certainly not enhanced.

Drugs

The relationship between the illicit production, traffic and use of drugs and the gravity of some social problems, including crime has always been sufficiently well established and has for almost a century demanded international attention. In some respects colonialism played a role in the widespread use of drugs in certain regions of the world. On the other hand, even before colonialism, drug addicition was common in a number of countries.

The first international conference on the control of narcotics was held in Shanghai in 1909 and led to the 1912 Convention, followed by the 1925 Convention concerning the manufacture, trade and preparation of drugs, the 1931 Convention on the Manufacture and Regulation of the Distribution of Narcotic Drugs, supplemented by the Agreement of 1931 on the suppression of opium smoking and the 1936 Convention for the Suppression of Illicit Traffic according to which governments were expected not only to enact appropriate penal measures but also to implement them effectively.

With the involvement of the United Nations, the confusion created by the conventions was partly reduced and the text updated by a Protocol signed at Lake Success, New York, in 1946. Eventually the Single Convention of 1961, which amalgamated all others, came into force in 1964 and was later supplemented by the Convention of Psychotropic Substances, adopted in 1971 and in force since 1976 which applies to hallucinogens, amphetamines, barbiturates, and so on. In 1972 the Single Convention was amended by a Protocol which came into force in 1975, highlighting the need for treatment and the rehabilitation of drug addicts.

The aims of these instruments are to limit the supply and demand of narcotic and psychotropic drugs to legitimate needs, to prevent and punish illicit production and traffic, to reduce drug addiction as much as possible and to keep pace with the new drugs.

A comparative study of the countries which are parties to these instruments and the reports of the Commission on Narcotic Drugs and other reliable sources of information shows:

(a) that a sizeable number of governments, particularly in developing countries, do not implement the provisions of the Conventions ratified and incorporated into their own national legislation;

(b) that in many countries high civil and military officials, sometimes government members, are deeply involved in the illicit production and traffic of drugs;

(c) that governmental corruption and organized crime are an essential part of these two activities and contribute to the increase of drug addiction; and

(d) that sometimes there is a close connection between ideological and revolutionary associations, organizations or groups and illicit production and traffic to finance their own ideological or political undertakings of which terrorism is often part.

The correlation between drug addition and crime has been asserted and denied at the national and international levels a number of times. Quite often research is conducted to demonstrate the correlation or to deny it. As a rule, in both cases theory and research have approached the relationship more from a causal-individualistic point of view than from a sociopolitical one, the latter meaning that society counts as much, if not more, than the individual in the consideration of the relationship. With some marked exceptions, the first approach is maintained in capitalist countries and the second in socialist countries. Curiously enough, outside of the latter quite often 'radicals' advocate in their own non-socialist countries the partial or total legalization of drug abuse.

At the 1971 meeting of the CCPC (doc. E/5191) the correlation between drugs and crime was discussed in some detail and it was stated that crimes were committed under the influence particularly of hallucinogens such as LSD, STP, and so on. More specifically the relationship between amphetamine abuse and aggressive behaviour was stressed, together with the fact that burglaries, robberies and frauds were committed to obtain drugs or money to get them. The frequent connection between users and the criminal milieu, especially but not only to obtain drugs, was also stressed. With respect to society's reaction, it was stated that in some countries there was a widespread fear of drug addicts. Other matters discussed were the economics of transnational illicit traffic and related criminal offences, the link between illicit traffic and organized crime, the role of law enforcement officers and of other sectors of the penal system, and the growing correlation between drug abuse, violation of human rights and crime.[1]

UNSDRI has published two research studies: *Investigating Drug Abuse* (1976), and *Policy and Research on Reduction of the Demand for Drugs* (1980). In the first, the following counter-motivating factors are listed, in decreasing order of importance: fear of intoxication; lack of need for drugs; a belief that the abuse of drugs was socially harmful; political convictions; and lack of opportunity. As motivating factors, also in decreasing order of importance: the desire to experience something new; curiosity; the desire to know oneself better; to escape from reality; lack of confidence; and the wish to become part of the group. It is also stated that in the majority of cases normal sexual habits prevail but that the incidence of homosexuality among addicts was three times higher than in any other group. Other conditioning factors of drug abuse were the relationship between the abuse of alcohol and that of drugs, family problems, imitation, publicity, ignorance of the danger involved and depression. The research also pointed out that addicts consume almost three times more alcohol than non-addicts and that there are more upper- and middle-class than lower-class people among them.

The second study reflects what has been found about the relationship between drug abuse and crime. While in some of the countries considered the relationship was stressed and specific reference was made to offences such as burglary and cheque forgery, the reports from others denied or minimized that relationship.

The matter was discussed at the Fifth Congress, in 1975, under the heading 'criminality associated with alcoholism and drug abuse'. It was agreed that alcohol was a drug, and that alcoholism was a major aspect of drug abuse, but that although criminality associated with alcohol and other drugs might involve many common characteristics, there were other and perhaps more significant aspects which separated them. It was stated that the introduction of narcotics and psychotropic substances into many countries represented a relatively new intrusion into and disruption of their cultures. Only rarely did alcoholics commit crimes in order to obtain alcohol or money to buy it, and such criminality was at a low level. The possession of narcotics and psychotropic substances, however, was usually illicit and the trafficking in them nearly always so. Therefore the criminality associated with those substances was concerned more with their transportation and with attempts to obtain them than with acts committed under their influence. Criminality connected with alcoholism was different from that connected with drug abuse. Specific reference was made to the international control system which effectively contributes to the prevention of illicit traffic and drug abuse. In this respect it was stressed that the penal provisions of the treaties distinguished between simple and serious offences and provided that only the latter should be liable to stringent punishment, particularly to penalties of deprivation of freedom. At any rate, a distinction should be made between the legal intervention against illicit producers, manufacturers and traffickers, and illicit possessor-consumers; for the latter non-penal forms of social control might sometimes be more appropriate. The treaties, if properly implemented, would achieve the aims assigned to them. From the discussion it became apparent that the most important areas in which action should be considered were illicit traffic, drug abuse, preventive measures, distinctions in the approaches taken by different countries and international drugs control.

The discussion clearly showed the difference of approach among the participants and even between the Branch and the representative of the Narcotics Division, the latter being in favour of a more constructive interpretation and implementation of the treaties. In its final recommendations the Congress did not make any reference to alcohol, and the main points of the recommendations concerning illicit traffic were the drafting of an international convention on judicial assistance and the improvement of extradition procedures on drug offences; that consideration should be given to transforming illicit traffic into a transnational criminal offence; that having been convicted in a country but made good an escape, drug offenders should serve their sentences in the country in which they are captured or take refuge; that international cooperation in every respect should be improved, that seized drugs should be destroyed; and that any national drug policy, such as the decriminalization of activities concerning *cannabis sativa*, should not adversely affect the drug control situation in neighbouring countries or at the international level.

In many respects the recommendations deserve full support but it is doubtful that the drafting of a new convention will improve the situation as long as members of governments, high civil and military officials, influential persons and many civil servants devote themselves to illicit production and traffic in a number of countries and benefit from total impunity in the vast majority of cases. The Congress did not consider this aspect which, without making specific mention of any country, fully justified a reference in the recommendations. By regarding alcohol as a drug and contemplating the 'liberalization' of the use of certain drugs, the Congress facilitated a greater consumption of alcohol inasmuch as drug addicts consume far more than non-addicts.

Following the general approach already mentioned, the Congress mostly regarded drug addiction as an individual condition deserving readaptation and not as a sociopolitical phenomenon requiring a different approach which, without excluding readaptation, subordinates it to sociopolitical considerations. According to the latter, drug addiction constitutes a serious danger to the general development of society: history clearly shows that when drug addiction or drug dependence have played a significant role in social habits, the country concerned never goes beyond an underdeveloped condition. The main question is how a country can really develop and maintain its developed condition if her leaders, high officials, professionals, scientists, employers and employees and many others directly participating in national development include a sizeable number of drug addicts. Would human rights, science and technology develop? What is the meaning of 'drug culture' which in the 1960s was proclaimed one of the aims of the cultural revolution? Can the tolerance to alcohol – which in some countries does not exist – be regarded as an argument to 'liberalize' drug addiction? In sum, can the existence of some social evils justify the introduction of a new one? Actually, as an instrument of power, drug addiction might be used in a subtle way to undermine resistance in a given country.

The answers to the above questions may be found in General Assembly resolutions 36/132 and 36/168,1981, which, after stressing the increase of illicit traffic and of the abuse of drugs, the links between drug trafficking and organized crime, illegal acquisition of arms and the growing exchange control violations as well as some forms of criminality, refer to the effects of drugs on the health and well-being of peoples and that they endanger national security and constitute a threat to the resilience and future of many countries. Consequently, member states are urged to develop more effective international cooperation and to support the international campaign against illicit production and traffic, and the drug abuse control strategy. As a supplement to both resolutions mention should be made of resolution 36/166, also of 1981, by which member states and other interested parties, including multinationals, are requested to cooperate more fully in providing data on banned or severely restricted substances so as to protect more effectively the social and humanitarian conditions of countries, particularly developing countries.

The correct non-permissive attitude of the socialist countries *vis-à-vis* drug abuse is widely known, and was attested at the 1982 session of ECOSOC which, at the request of the representative of a European socialist country, adopted resolution 1982/10 by which the organization of an International Year against Drug Addiction was decided. It is hoped that this Year will offer a good opportunity to examine the harmful socioeconomic and political effects of drug addiction.[2]

Although summarily examined, it is clear that in its triple aspect of illicit production, traffic, and drug abuse, the drugs problem is extremely complex and closely related to many forms of crime in which corruption at every governmental or official level plays a role. Both complexity and criminality might be considerably reduced if the governments concerned acted with a sense of national and international responsibility which, judging by the reports of the Commission on Narcotic Drugs, is not as frequent as it should be.

If, as suggested, illicit production and traffic become a transnational offence, it is difficult to see how the question of the criminal responsibility of the state, still denied by some, could be avoided. An objective consideration of the growth of illicit production and traffic and the frequent conniving in both of governments, leads to the conclusion that they are becoming part and parcel of the list of crimes against mankind so often perpetrated nowadays but so seldom appearing in criminal statistics. *Mutatis mutandis,* the same applies to the 'liberalization' of drug abuse regarded by its advocates as part of a 'progressive' way of thinking.

Slavery and related matters

Probably to many people slavery is an obsolete criminal policy matter, but in fact it is more important than it was owing to new varieties of it facilitated by the growing number of refugees, displaced, exiled and stateless persons, many forms of discrimination (of which apartheid is the most significant), inhuman conditions in some penal labour camps, exploitation of migrant or 'imported' workers, trade in persons (particularly women and children), and in some cases forced prostitution. The crimes resulting from these activities are piracy, murder, bodily injury, sexual offences and an increasing number of criminal violations of human rights. These and related offences are seldom officially reported. Many are concentrated in certain regions of the world, the most significant being South-East Asia.

The suppression of slavery was initiated in the nineteenth century, and at the Vienna Congress of 1815 eight countries adopted a Declaration advocating the 'universal abolition of slavery' which, like many other declarations, was ignored even by some of the countries proclaiming it. In 1919 a Convention was adopted according to which the colonial powers should protect the native populations, improve their living conditions and suppress slavery. The mandate system, introduced by the League of Nations, raised the slavery question again and after some discussion it was decided that whatever the category of mandate (there were three categories: A, B and C) any convention against slavery should apply to them. In 1922 the League set up a Commission, the two reports of which were used in the drafting of the 1926 Convention which defines slavery as 'the status or condition of a person over whom any or all the powers attaching to the right of ownership are exercised'. This broad definition, coupled with the definition of slave trade given by the same Convention, and certain provisions of the 1956 United Nations Supplementary Convention, means that other institutions and practices should be regarded, if not as slavery, certainly as slavery practices. Mohammed Awad's *Report on Slavery* (United Nations, 1966), shows that in spite of the shortcomings inherent in the questionnaire system, particularly when addressed to governments, slavery and the slave trade were at that time widely practised in some Arab and African countries. Certainly during the discussion which took place at ECOSOC, the governments affected denied the charges, particularly those brought by the Anti-Slavery Society, which substantiated all of them while those 'charged' were not able to submit data in rebuttal. Similar to slavery and then still practised particularly in some Latin American countries, was the placing of children by their parents or guardians with prosperous people in return for a small payment. Although the practice was regarded as a criminal offence, it was frequent in countries with large sectors of Indian populations. In all probability, this practice has now practically disappeared but the same cannot be said of old and new forms of forced labour. Nowadays illegal workers, refugees, exiled, displaced, expelled and persecuted as well as other mass exodus persons, offer ample human material for slavery-like practices and victimization in many countries. In any case the growing number of resolutions concerning the conditions enumerated above clearly show that the problem is far more serious than it was twenty years ago.[3]

Analysis of the sources mentioned and others too numerous to be cited allows the following remarks:

(a) Slavery and slavery-like practices have a long historical past often mixed with cruel, inhuman or degrading treatment and crime.

(b) Although Western colonialism was largely responsible for the increase of slavery and the slave trade in the nineteenth century, long before this both were practised in some Arab and African regions. In fact the Western slave trade would hardly have been possible without the greed of many Arab and African chieftains and traders.

(c) Contemporary slavery-like practices are greatly facilitated by the frequent mass exodus of refugees, migrant workers, and exiled and displaced persons as a result of political instability, ideological persecution, disguised or open military occupation or support of dictatorial regimes, widespread poor economic living conditions and discrimination of many kinds among which apartheid is one of the most inhuman.

Treatment of offenders

The treatment of offenders has been one of the most discussed subjects of UN criminal policy, due partly to the importance attached to the rehabilitation of offenders and partly to the highly unsatisfactory condition of institutional treatment in most countries.

The number of documents dealing with the subject is still increasing since it is dealt with not only by the United Nations but also by some of the specialized agencies and a good number of non-governmental organizations. Sometimes the same subject is discussed on several occasions partly due to the indifference of governments to taking into account what was forwarded to them as the basis for a national policy. In others the discussions try to put forward some Western approaches which, although usually commendable, cannot gain general acceptance inasmuch as the treatment of offenders must take into account various national characteristics provided they do not conflict with human rights and the minimum standards set up by the UN.

Since 1948 the UN has been trying to improve the institutional and non-institutional treatment of prisoners which, for all practical purposes, embraces more than convicted offenders, but the results are still far below what they should be mostly due to the proliferation of dictatorial regimes all over the world. Quite often these regimes institute special procedures which ignore the minimum standards demanded by the UN in the treatment of suspects, detainees, arrested, imprisoned and convicted offenders. The above means that the term 'treatment' may refer to the way in which criminal justice is understood, or alternatively to the way people are treated in a penal or equivalent institution. The first aspect is dealt with later when criminal justice is discussed, the second here: since not all the numerous aspects of treatment can be examined separately they have been grouped under the following sub-items: Standard Minimum Rules; prison architecture; prison labour; special types of offender; and non-institutional treatment of offenders. Needless to say, all of them are closely connected to criminal justice aims, procedures and practices.

Standard Minimum Rules for the Treatment of Prisoners
As already stated, the formulation of these Rules was initiated by the IPPC and the League of Nations but it was at the First UN Congress, in Geneva in 1955, that the text prepared by the Secretariat was discussed and eventually adopted. In 1957, in compliance with ECOSOC resolution 663 C (XXIV), the Rules were forwarded to all governments for their consideration and implementation.

The basic principles of the Rules are that not all are applicable in all places and at all times, but they represent the minimum conditions which are accepted as suitable by the UN. They do not preclude experiment and other practices provided these are in harmony with the principles and purposes of the Rules. This sensible twofold aim has not always been understood by those advocating 'modernization' of the Rules, by which they mean what is done in their own countries; what is regarded as advanced in one country is not necessarily a model for all others. As stated, the Rules constitute a minimum which, curiously enough, is not always observed by some developed countries in which, among other serious shortcomings, overcrowding is frequent. The same applies to those countries which, while not providing information of any sort, maintain that their prison systems are well above the Rules; an assertion which is belied by the frequently appalling conditions prevailing in their labour or detention camps.

Other basic principles are that the Rules should be applied impartially without discrimination, that untried prisoners should be kept apart from those convicted, young offenders from adult offenders and women from men, that in every place where persons are imprisoned there shall be kept a bound register with numbered pages in which shall be entered in respect of each person all information concerning his or her identity, the reasons for committal and the day and hour of admission and release. If such minimum provisions had been observed everywhere there is little doubt that the fate of many 'missing' persons would be ascertained.

The modernization of the SMR and the desire, expressed particularly at the Fourth and Fifth Congresses, to ensure their better application and implementation, are merely a delaying tactic on the part of some member states. Others argue that because the SMR were adopted in 1955, they did not have the opportunity to participate in their formulation, the implication being that they are therefore not bound by them. But this makes little sense. By the same token those members are not obliged to comply with other UN resolutions, with the Universal Declaration of Human Rights or the Charter itself.

At the Sixth Congress in 1980, the Secretariat submitted a working paper, *The Implementation of the United Nations Standard Minimum Rules for the Treatment of Offenders* (A/CONF.87/11,1980), which should be studied in conjunction with two others, *Human Rights and Criminal Justice: Recent Developments (1975–1980)* (A/CONF. 87/BP/5,1980) and *United Nations Norms and Guidelines in Criminal Justice* (A/CONF.87/9,1980) – all three extremely useful. The first inquiry on the implementation of the Rules was conducted in 1967: only 44 government replies were received, the analysis of which showed that the situation was highly unsatisfactory in the majority of countries. The contributions to issue no. 36 of the *International*

Review of Criminal Policy, (1967), also confirmed this in spite of some attempts to present a better picture. The second inquiry was conducted in 1974; 62 answers were received, the analysis of which was not very encouraging and the matter was discussed, as indicated, at the Fifth Congress. In 1976 the CCPC drafted a new rule (no. 95), which specifically extended the application of the Rules to all persons arrested or imprisoned with or without charge or conviction and also a set of procedures for the effective implementation of the Rules (doc. E/CN.5/536); the work thus done by the CCPC was welcomed by General Assembly resolution 31/85,1976 in which, *inter alia*, ECOSOC was invited to consider with due priority the recommendations made by the CCPC; accordingly by its resolution 2076 (LXII) 1977, ECOSOC adopted the text of rule no. 95 which is as follows:

> Without prejudice to the provisions of article 9 of the International Covenant on Civil and Political Rights, persons arrested or imprisoned without charge shall be accorded the same protection as that accorded under part I and part II, section C. Relevant provisions of part II, section A, shall likewise be applicable where their application may be conducive to the benefit of this special group of persons in custody, provided that no measures shall be taken implying that reeducation or rehabilitation is in any way appropriate to persons not convicted of any criminal offence.

ECOSOC did not have time to consider the procedures for the effective implementation of the Rules as proposed by the CCPC, which are included in the annex to the working paper mentioned above. Briefly, the procedures prescribe that all states are requested to adopt and apply the Rules subject to their adaptation and harmonization with the laws and culture of the adopting state, but without deviation from the spirit and purpose of the Rules; when adopted, the SMR should be made available to all persons under detention, member states shall inform the Secretary-General regularly of the extent of implementation, the information received should be disseminated by the Secretary-General, technical assistance shall be provided to governments asking for it and the regional institutes shall develop curricula and training material based on the SMR. If account is taken of the fact that some of the procedures impose responsibilities on governments which many of them have dexterously avoided, it is not surprising that ECOSOC had no time to discuss the matter, which remains dormant.

The Implementation of the United Nations Standard Minimum Rules for the Treatment of Offenders is interesting not only because of the answers received and the modest quality of some of them but also for the persistent absence of answers from some governments. The questionnaire was sent in October 1979, with a follow-up in January 1980. By May 1980, only 38 governments had replied, or barely 25 per cent of United Nations membership. Only one European socialist country, Romania, answered, and the analysis shows that some of the assertions made by certain countries are contradicted by other UN information on torture, cruel, inhuman or degrading treatment or punishment, missing persons, and so on. Such is the case, among others, with the answers from Argentina, Chile, Guatemala and Uruguay. As for many of the non-responding countries, their silence cannot always be interpreted as a satisfactory application of the Rules.

The main conclusions which may be obtained from the working papers cited are that the Rules have had a significant impact on the laws and practices of many countries but little if anything can be said about a greater number of them, particularly concerning accommodation, separation of categories, sanitary conditions and other fundamental minima set up by the Rules. In the best of cases only 60 per cent of the answers give the impression that the Rules are applied more or less satisfactorily. More specifically, the Secretariat states that from the answers received it is impossible to establish whether the replies reflect actual practice or not, that there is a lack of basic comparable data on current prison trends and on the ways of dealing with offenders, and that a sample of only 38 countries for the entire world is not representative.

The Sixth Congress, to which the above three working papers were submitted, did not discuss the unsolved matter of the implementation of the Rules in the vast majority of countries. Actually the subject was avoided and instead some resolutions, namely nos. 8, 9, 10, 13 and 14, dealing with related matters, were adopted. The first refers to alternatives to imprisonment which had been discussed in full at the Second Congress in 1960, and to a large extent at the Fifth in 1975. The fact is that this subject cannot really be solved as long as the Rules are not implemented to a reasonable extent. About resolution 9 on the needs of women prisoners enough has already been said. As for resolution 10 on the social resettlement of prisoners, here again the implementation of the Rules is a fundamental prerequisite. It is difficult to see how governments will comply with the invitation in the resolution to inform the Secretary-General about resettlement, and still more how the CCPC will consider the question of the development of measures for resettlement in the context of the revision of the SMR which is little more than a delaying tactic for not implementing them.

As for the transfer of offenders suggested by resolution 13, which really refers to prisoners, the matter was discussed at the Fifth Congress where reference was made to the fact that in all probability Turkey had been the pioneer country in the matter by passing a law in 1964 – partly based on the draft prepared by this author as UN Adviser – by which bilateral agreements may be reached with any interested country. Also at the Fifth Congress specific references were made to the need for the prisoner's consent. Although only slow progress is being made, the system is developing in Europe and America. Finally, resolution 14, after making a passing reference to the SMR, insists on the implementation of human rights instruments for the benefit of prisoners which cannot easily be envisaged as long as the Rules are not applied.

A *Model Agreement on the Transfer of Foreign Prisoners* (E/AC.57/ 1984,7) was submitted by the Secretary-General to the CCPC at its 1984 session but lack of time prevented a full discussion. Following the recommendation of the Fifth Committee 'in order to facilitate the return to their domicile of persons serving their sentences in foreign countries, policies and practices should be developed by utilizing regional cooperation and starting with bilateral arrangements' (A/CONF.87/8), the Secretariat elaborated for the consideration of the Sixth Congress some broad principles which, after discussion, led to resolution 13 urging the adoption of procedures whereby such transfers may be effected.

The report on the model agreement examines many of the questions involved, and makes the good point that the development of transfer agreements cannot solve all the problems, as there would always be a period of time before an individual could be transferred, as well as a certain number of prisoners who would not want to be transferred. The report also states that relevant sections of the SMR should be applied in a pragmatic and flexible way in order to ensure equal treatment to all prisoners. The annex to the report contains the resolution adopted at the seminar on the subject organized in Vienna in 1983 by the Vienna Alliance of NGOs as well as a draft model agreement.

The subject raises too many questions to be discussed here. Suffice it to say that the priority granted by the draft to the sentencing or the administering state is not fully justified if the proliferation of dictatorial regimes is kept in mind, as well as the doubtful validity of the term 'sovereignty' in many cases. Another objection is that in spite of the guarantees stipulated, the transfer may be transformed into a hidden extradition for offences previously committed which, in view of the proliferation of dictatorial regimes, cannot be justified.

Analysis of the reports on the regional preparatory meetings for the Seventh Congress, submitted at the 1984 session of the CCPC,

shows that although the SMR are already largely embodied in th
penitentiary legislation of many countries, this is not so in others
although reference to them is made in national or regional training
courses. Generally the factors preventing a satisfactory application
of the fundamental rules are the increase of prison populations, which
in most cases means overcrowding even in some developed countries
lack of financial means; shortage of trained personnel; and, although
not specifically mentioned, political instability and the lack of interest
of dictatorial regimes in improving institutional and non-institutional
treatment. More specific factors are the extensive use of imprison
ment or detention pending trial in many countries, particularly fo
political prisoners; delays in criminal procedure; difficulties in trans
ferring detainees; and incarceration of fine defaulters for shor
periods of time – a category which, in some countries, constitute
a large percentage of the prison population.

Closely related to the SMR are the recommendations adopted
by the 1955 Congress on the selection and training of personne
in correctional institutions and open and penal correctional institu
tions. The first requires that institutional personnel should b
regarded as performing a social service demanding ability, training
good teamwork, and specialization; that the service should have a
civil status and not a military or paramilitary one; and that personne
should possess suitable intelligence. As for the open institutions
the recommendations are that their characteristics are the absenc
of material or physical precautions against escape; that they should
be governed by a system based on self-discipline; and that the
should be independent of other establishments.[4]

Although in some developing countries the recommendations ar
being applied and in others steps are being taken for their gradua
implementation, the situation is not satisfactory. In some region
frequent training courses are available, and attended by a growing
number of prison personnel, but by themselves training and oper
institutions cannot yield the results expected as long as the SMF
are not implemented as they should be.

Related to the SMR in more than one aspect are the alternative
to imprisonment which were partly discussed at the Fifth Congress
under 'the treatment of offenders, in custody or in the community
with special reference to the implementation of the Standard Mini
mum Rules' and at the Sixth Congress which adopted resolution
no. 8 on alternatives to imprisonment recommending member state
to introduce such alternatives, and requesting the Secretary-Genera
and the CCPC to provide advice and support.

At the 1984 session of the CCPC the Secretary-General submitted
a report, *Alternatives to Imprisonment and Measures for the Socia*

Resettlement of Prisoners (E/AC.57/1984,9). In preparing the report, the Secretary-General sent member and non-member states a note requesting relevant information. The analysis of the 53 replies shows that the most usual alternatives are fines, suspension of sentence, probation, corrective or compulsory labour and community service. As for social resettlement, the report stresses the crucial importance of the release stage and the role of education or vocational training, the non-interruption of personal contacts, the cooperation of official and private organizations, accommodation in halfway houses, pre-release assistance and availability of adequate personnel. The report ends by suggesting that since the public is particularly sensitive to this subject, it should be adequately informed and made aware of the importance of the new trends in crime prevention and the treatment of offenders.

As part of the humane treatment of offenders and non-offenders, the emerging roles of the police and other law enforcement agencies were discussed at the Fifth Congress. The main questions examined were police professionalism and accountability, recruitment and training, police responses to changing forms of criminality, police–community relations, private security organizations, police involvement in the formulation of legislation, international cooperation and the present and future role of the police. The Congress did an excellent job on the subject and eventually the Code of Conduct for Law Enforcement Officials was adopted by General Assembly resolution 34/169,1979, asking governments to give favourable consideration to the Code within the framework of national legislation. Subsequently, the General Assembly passed resolution 35/170,1980, inviting the CCPC to study the application of the Code, taking as a basis the information received from member states. Accordingly, the latter were invited to submit information on the implementation of the Code. The report on the replies was submitted to the CCPC at its 1984 session but again lack of time prevented the detailed discussion it deserved. Only 29 members, or less than 19 per cent of the UN membership, answered. The small percentage is a significant indicator not only of the situation in many countries, but also of the chronic lack of cooperation of many governments as far as criminal policy is concerned.

An analysis of the report (E/AC.57,1984,4) shows far too many responses with no factual information about the difficulties in the implementation of the Code. When compared with other UN documents concerning torture, cruel, inhuman or degrading treatment or punishment, 'missing persons', summary executions, illegal arrest or detention and related matters, some of the answers sound, to say the least, unconvincing. The main conclusion is that often 'implementation' is understood simply as the incorporation into the national legislation of some relevant provisions of the Code, or that the Code is referred to or explained at training courses for police officers. But between legislative insertion and training and actual observance of the Code there is a wide gap.

Prison architecture

While institutional treatment has been discussed from every angle, the prison or penal institution in which that treatment is supposed to take place has received scanty attention. Yet the effectiveness of any programme depends to a great extent on the characteristics and ambiance of the institution in which it is applied.

Putting aside passing references to prison architecture and internal surroundings when discussing other related matters (one of the last occasions being the Fifth Congress in 1975, when major economic and social consequences of crime were considered), and putting aside also the references made by the SMR when dealing with accommodation and other matters, the first meeting at which prison architecture was discussed was probably the First United Nations Consultative Group, held in Geneva in 1961, at which prison construction was considered in some detail. The Secretariat submitted a report, *Planning and Construction,* which, although mostly concerned with the treatment of juveniles and young offenders, made general references among which the following should be mentioned: too often institutions were designed having in mind the most difficult kind of inmate; the preoccupation with security is often not only wasteful but detrimental to prisoners, for the bulk of whom security institutions are unjustified; mass treatment should be avoided and institutions designed to maximize certain services and minimize others; in all probability prison populations would become younger almost everywhere; institutions should be able to make use of nearby public utilities; the surroundings and the inside of the prison should make the passing of time as bearable as possible; the erection of a complex of institutions has a considerable appeal in some countries; the type of building should reflect some social ideals and represent a humane balance between security, re-education and the needs of treatment. Although some of the considerations were too general, no doubt to meet different opinions, and others reflected a rather limited conception of crime, they deserve attention inasmuch as all try to demonstrate the close relationship between treatment and physical surroundings quite often overlooked or ignored by governments or administrators mostly due to the lack of a planned criminal policy.

The idea of constructing large institutions and complexes was firmly opposed by several countries, among them Belgium, Denmark and Norway, but supported by others, particularly Poland and the Ukraine. The reason given by the latter was that 'only large prisons facilitate the organization of productive work', a reasoning which can easily be contested by the fact that if prison labour is integrated with local, regional and national labour it does not need to be organized on a large scale. The crux of the matter lies in what is understood by 'productive labour' and whether it is not sometimes identified with forced labour.

It was said that architects seldom understand prison matters, and therefore even modern prison architecture is obviously at fault externally and internally. The remark is correct but it also applies to many prison administrators or services. In some developed countries huge prisons and complexes are still built far beyond the maximum recommended capacity of 500 occupants, which was regarded by many, when the SMR were discussed, as excessive. In some countries like the USA such institutions are often called 'facilities', which is little more than a euphemism.

It is this kind of institution and institutionalization which has contributed to the deinstitutionalization movement, which is certainly justified in some respects, and to the acceptance of the expression 'residual prisoner' unfortunately adopted by the Secretariat. The fact that prisoners are kept in prison does not mean that they are residual in any way, and still less that penal institutions are unnecessary.

In many countries prison construction is becoming a serious concern: in some, old buildings are still used and often overcrowding is the rule. The fact is that no planning of the penal system has been attempted in the vast majority of countries. The problem has been aggravated by the increasing number of prisoners awaiting trial, sometimes for long periods of time. The situation is still worse in the local jails where a large proportion of the prison population is kept, both as detainees and convicted.

The construction and upkeep of prisons is becoming ever more expensive, partly due to rising costs of materials and the need to construct them in accordance with human rights standards and treatment requirements. The problem must be faced that even putting aside the question of detainees, the prison population of the immediate future will increase for the simple reason that violent crime will also increase, and the myth of the rehabilitation of the offender will eventually be replaced by the protection of society in accordance with fundamental collective human rights. In other words, the cost of criminal justice will increase, a fact which should be taken into account by UN criminal policy.

Prison labour

As part of the general subject of treatment, prison labour has been discussed at length at the international level, though with scanty practical results as far as the prisoners, their families, victims and above all criminal justice are concerned. With some Western exceptions, prison labour is barely organized, and in certain countries it is identified with correctional labour which in most cases means the inhuman exploitation of convicted prisoners.

In 1932 the ILO conducted a survey, but only 27 countries answered the questionnaire and not all the answers were as complete as they should have been: with some exceptions, the conclusion was that prison labour was in very poor shape. In 1935–7 the IPPC conducted another survey and 29 governments answered: improvements were shown in some countries but the previous highly unsatisfactory situation remained in most of them. In 1950 at the Hague Congress, the last organized by the IPPC, the discussion of 'how is prison labour to be organized so as to yield both moral benefit and a useful social economic return' attested again that theoretical assertions were dominant, that some countries were still in favour of the old approaches and that prison labour was not always available.

In 1952 the question was raised at the United Nations by the Section of Social Defence before the then Social Commission. The Commission refused the priority requested, but the Section was persistent and finally the Commission granted it. Consequently in 1953 a questionnaire was sent to all member states, and 38 answers were received. The USSR did not answer since at that time she was openly opposed to UN criminal policy.

The main purposes of the inquiry were to obtain government information on the systems used in the organization of prison labour, its place in the public works field, the occupational background of prisoners, post-release employment opportunities, the implementation of social measures, protection, and kinds and amount of remuneration. Not all the answers were complete or reliable, but the fact that the resulting report by Professor Ralph England, of the Department of Sociology at the University of Pennsylvania, was prepared in the Section itself, explains that in spite of its shortcomings the text was regarded by many as a good piece of work.

The main points made were that the extent of prison labour used in public works was impossible to ascertain because the countries concerned evaded any clear answer; the state-use system was predominant everywhere, though sometimes other systems such as lease contract, piece-price and others were used; the organization and availability of prison work was by no means what it should be even in some well-developed countries; the remuneration was far below that for free labour; generally trade unions opposed any expansion or improvement of prison labour; overmanned occupational work for the maintenance of the institution, sometimes called 'broom-leaning work' was widespread particularly in some well-developed countries; and in some developing countries what was called prison administration was very poor.

More specifically the report showed that only in some European countries were regular wages paid to prisoners of certain categories, and that only Yugoslavia paid it to all of them. In some cases the answers stated that the remuneration paid was as much as possible or that every effort was made to pay it. Very few countries granted indemnity for work-related injury or illness, and in most cases it was *ex gratia*. The situation was worse in the developing countries. Safety conditions were seldom what they should be.

The SMR say that for sentenced prisoners prison labour is required but must not be of an afflictive nature; that sufficient useful work as well as vocational training shall be provided; that the organization and methods shall resemble as closely as possible those of similar outside work; that the precautions laid down to protect the safety and health of free workers shall be equally observed in prison; that provision shall be made to indemnify prisoners against industrial injury or disease on terms no less favourable than those extended to free workmen; and that the remuneration shall be equitable.

In 1957 the ILO Convention on the Abolition of Forced Labour was adopted and is still in force. According to its provisions forced labour is prohibited and shall not be used as a coercion or as a political educational measure, sanction, discriminatory or disciplinary measure or for economic development. Nowadays there is sufficient data about many countries to conclude that all these prohibitions are ignored by them. Otherwise the question of cruel, inhuman or degrading treatment or punishment would barely have arisen.

At the Second Congress, in London in 1960, the integration of prison labour with the national economy, including remuneration of prisoners, was discussed on the basis of two reports, one prepared by J. Carlos García Basalo, a UN expert, and the other by the Secretariat. The main points made by both reports are that such integration was not an easy matter, partly because of the problems of free labour, and partly because prison labour was often regarded as an aspect of treatment; the remuneration of prison labour did not exist in some countries or was resisted in others for not very convincing reasons; the upkeep of institutions was always needed and often must be regarded as work, but it is not easy to integrate it with the national economy; and finally the integration of any labour with the national economy raised questions which required very careful consideration.

In its conclusions, however, the London Congress declared that the prisoner is a worker deprived of freedom; that prison labour should be regarded as a normal and regular activity of the free man and also as an integral part of institutional treatment; and that prison labour must be suited to the natural capacities, character and if possible, preferences of the individual so as to prepare him for normal life. Further, the following points were made: the need for vocational training; that the state shall ensure the full employment of the able-bodied prisoner as well as his individual placement in semi-liberty; that the organization of prison labour and the compensation for accident or illness should be similar to that of free labour; that in countries where labour planning or cooperative management exist both systems should be taken into account in the integration of prison labour with the national economy; that the number of prisoners assigned to unskilled maintenance work for which qualifications are not required must be reduced to the essential minimum; that according to rule 76 equitable remuneration should be paid; and that the final aim should be the payment of normal remuneration equivalent to that of a free worker provided output is the same both in quantity and quality.

Since the Second Congress prison labour has not been discussed; the impression one gains is that it is carefully avoided by the representatives of many governments. The silence, however, does not mean that the situation has improved in most countries. On the contrary, the existing data show that in many of them, particularly where dictatorial regimes prevail, prison labour has seriously deteriorated. In other countries national economic difficulties make the subject unpopular even among professionals. Here and there some prisons are exhibited as models in all respects including prison labour, but such exceptions, sometimes more apparent than real, confirm the general unsatisfactory situation.

The difficulties of improving the situation are enormous and in all probability the growth of prison populations in most countries, the increase of maintenance and construction costs everywhere, and the rapid deterioration of the national economy in many countries will not only prevent integration but also the more modest purpose of providing useful prison work which is decently paid.

Many of the decisions of the London Congress are praiseworthy, particularly as far as the correlation between criminal policy and national development is concerned. Without entering into details, suffice it to say that even in well-developed countries already in the 1950s and still more nowadays the state is not able to provide full employment for every able-bodied free worker, and still less for every prisoner. The assertion that in the majority of cases the prisoner is a worker is not quite correct, and certainly has been continuously contested particularly in the developed countries by the trade unions which often do their best to reduce to a minimum, if not to abolish, production or industry within prisons. The most recent case is that of the United Kingdom where in March 1983 under trade union pressure a bill was introduced according to which the 'unfair competition by prison industry' should be dealt with. According to the statements made, prison industry contributed to the high cost of 'rehabilitatory work in prisons' and the maximum earnings (the term wages has always been avoided) of the inmates working in prison industries is £4.25 a week. Certainly the increase of unemployment, the economic crisis, the complaints of 'civilian firms' and other factors may explain all this but to explain is not necessarily to justify.

It may be argued that none of this takes place in those countries in which, owing to their socioeconomic structure, full employment is maintained. Close scrutiny of data shows that often what is presented as full employment is no more than overemployment. In any case the governments concerned refuse to make data available concerning the type of work, working hours and conditions, remuneration paid, and so on.

In sum, in spite of the efforts made by the United Nations, the question of prison labour remains unsolved in the vast majority of countries. New approaches are needed which should be sought in the close relationship between the planning of criminal justice and penal systems and that of national development, on the understanding that that relationship does not mean a surrender of the first two to the aims of economic development.

Special types of offenders

Discussion of this subject has taken place mostly at European Consultative Group meetings, in Geneva in 1956 and 1958; at the Strasbourg meeting, in 1957, jointly organized with the Council of Europe; at the Copenhagen meeting, in 1958, with the cooperation of the WHO; and, in a wider geographical context, at the Third Congress, in 1965. Since then incidental references to special types of offenders may be found in some documents. The fact that the recommendations were adopted with some exceptions by representatives of European countries in no way reduces their obvious value.

The special groups discussed were the mentally abnormal offender, the habitual offender, the sexual offender and the young adult offender. The recidivist, so closely related to all of them, was taken into account when recidivism was discussed at the Third Congress.[5]

All groups, particularly the abnormal, habitual and sexual, are so closely related that sometimes the three conditions appear in the same kind of offender. Papers were prepared by members of the European Consultative Group on the three types, data gathered, even in some cases from non-European countries, and programmes and policies recommended, the scientific and practical value of which is still manifest. What follows is a summary.

Abnormal offenders. It was stated that from the legal and psychiatric points of view the concept of the abnormal offender was far from clear. Every offender is assumed to be normal and responsible, and only those suffering from some serious mental disorders are regarded as irresponsible. In some cases habitual offending is a characteristic, and sexual offenders are relatively frequent among mentally abnormal offenders. These relationships do not mean that all habitual and sexual offenders are abnormal or vice versa but that, as stated, all three types are sometimes closely related or coincide in the same person.

The terms 'insane', 'mentally deficient', etc., are often used as equivalents but the equivalence is only relative. Moreover, the mental anomaly or abnormality may not be permanent or constant or affect every aspect of human behaviour. Although frequently used, the expressions 'irresistible impulse', 'delinquent by tendency', 'diminished responsibility', and many others, refer to situations or conditions which should be carefully considered before a conclusion is reached. In any case, generalizations should be avoided. The term 'psychopath' was often criticised.

Although serious attempts were made to reach agreement on some concepts, no standard definitions were adopted beyond that of considering abnormal offenders as those suffering from mental abnormality which is usually subdivided into insanity and abnormality. The understanding was that even the term 'normal' is not a clear cut concept.

At the Copenhagen meeting the question of psychiatric treatment of accused persons received particular attention and Dr E.A. Babayan from the USSR submitted a paper in which he said that psychiatric examination of offenders may be requested by the public prosecutor or the investigating authorities as well as by the accused himself, his relatives or counsel. His assertion that compulsory psychiatric treatment was not a penal sanction was significant. His colleague, Dr G. Morozov, no less forcibly stressed the active role played by human consciousness or people's ability to control their actions through the knowledge of the laws of objective reality, the conclusion being that every person is, in principle, responsible for his actions, a principle which, according to him, lies at the root of Soviet legislation on responsibility.

Habitual offenders. It was stated that tramps, beggars, habitual petty offenders and what are sometimes called 'offenders by inclination', should be excluded from the concept of the habitual offender. Rather, by habitual was understood the offender who has committed offences in sufficient number and gravity as to suggest that he may be a danger to society; the offender who has already served sufficient sentences to suggest that he will not respond to normal penal measures whether or not institutional; the offender who, from the study of his personality and of his social history, seems likely to persist in the commission of offences and therefore constitutes a danger to society; and finally, anyone who, in view of the foregoing conclusions, appears to the court as a person to whom special measures should be applied for the protection of society. Actually, all four described conditions quite often merge and the last one implies the judicial consideration of the others.

It was added that the law should lay down the cases and circumstances in which special measures shall be applied by specifying the number of previous offences and the nature of the offences or convictions or the sentences served.

Sexual offenders. Among others the following questions were discussed: whether or not sexual offences always imply the commission of a sexual act; the misuse of physical or undue psychological pressure in the commission of sexual offences; the seduction of minors, dependents and unprotected persons; rape, indecent assault, incest and acts against public decency. It was stated that there was no reason to make a distinction between sexual and non-sexual offences as far as criminal proceedings were concerned, that many sexual offences were of a minor character, that from a psychiatric point of view sexual offenders constitute a heterogeneous group with a wide range of personalities, that there is no reason to believe that specialized care is needed for a high proportion of sexual offenders, that sex crime is apt to arouse great emotional reactions, and that the public should not be confused by terms which suggest that the crime was more serious than it actually was.

The harmful effects upon the victim vary widely and law enforcement and judicial procedure should be designed and applied so as to spare the victim and witnesses further emotional harm. Medical, psychological, sociological or other assistance for the victim and victim's family should be provided whenever necessary and possible. The segregation of sexual offenders from society should not be encouraged any more than that of other offenders. It was also stated that many persons with sexual problems can be helped with medical, psychiatric or other treatment, and that the prevention of sex offences lies in the field of general mental health as well as in applied sociology, sexual education and community attitudes.

Recidivist offenders. The subject was discussed at the Third Congress in 1965, where its increase in many countries and the need for effective preventive measures were stressed. According to some participants one of the most marked conditioning factors of the increase was institutional treatment which should be replaced as much as possible by non-institutional treatment. It was said that those who are sent to prisons or correctional institutions tend to become recidivists by committing more offences than before. This kind of simplified reasoning, at that time favoured particularly by some Nordic European countries, was objected to by others who more sensibly and objectively made a distinction between institutional treatment and the conditions in which it is carried out in many countries including developed ones.

What was far more interesting was that during the discussions specific reference was made to crimes against peace and mankind, the implication being that in those crimes recidivism was frequent and that imprisonment was the right measure to be taken. Unfortunately, most of the offenders involved are never sent to prison since many of them are members of the armed forces who, as a rule, evade any kind of penal sanction.

Close scrutiny of the discussions shows that those advocating the reduction or even the abolition of institutional treatment had in mind only some of the forms of common crime while those opposing such a narrow conception, which curiously enough was still regarded by many as progressive, took into account a wider idea of the extent of crime in which official, semi-official, ideological, economic and other varieties were already manifest, and are at present more significant than the traditional kinds of common crime. On the other hand, the impact of the abuse of detention, arrest, long periods of imprisonment pending trial and other serious shortcomings of the majority of the penal systems often have a serious effect on the increase of recidivism.

Young adult offenders. The recognition of young adult offenders as a separate group from juvenile and adult offenders was at that time one of the aims advocated by numerous criminologists, not all of them fully aware of the difficulties involved in making the distinction, and of the artificial nature of the distinction once made.

Among European countries the distinction was not easy since the upper age limit for juvenile offenders ranged from 16 to 21 years. It was suggested that the young adult offender required specific types of treatment under civil law, under criminal law whether in freedom or in institutions, and under supervision and after-care when released. As regards treatment under civil law, it was reported that if the prosecutor agrees, the young adult should be brought before the civil judge or a social authority who may place him under supervision and care of a special organization which takes particular interest in his home conditions, and so on. As regards forms of treatment under criminal law the following were examined: fines, probation, suspended sentences, attendance centres, reparation, contributions, short- and long-term treatment and other related measures which may in fact all be applied to juvenile as well as to adult offenders. It was suggested that the court should decide both the choice of treatment and the kind of institution to which the young adult would be sent by the prison administration. With respect to capital punishment, it was decided that the issue involved a full prior discussion of that sanction, and therefore it was inadvisable to discuss whether or not it may be applied to young adult offenders.

Comments. While the suggestions concerning mentally abnormal, habitual and sexual offenders on the whole maintain their validity and may be used as solid foundations for a corresponding contemporary criminal policy, those on recidivism raise a number of objections, some of them already pointed out. It may be added that the complexity of crime as a sociopolitical phenomenon, a condition which has always existed but has in most cases been ignored by a conservative Western criminology, embraces far more than the traditional kinds of common crime and therefore has a kind of recidivism quite different from that contemplated by that criminology. As for sexual offences, contemporary sexual permissiveness in many countries favours the impunity of most of them but has not reduced the victimization in the vast majority of cases. In some Western countries so-called sexual freedom is frequently advocated and regarded as 'progress' and in some, like Sweden, even the decriminalization of incest is contemplated. The question is whether 'sexual freedom' should be regarded as an absolute individual right. The answer is in the negative, and in this respect the socialist countries give an example which is unfortunately ignored by the permissive attitude prevailing in a number of capitalist ones. There is no doubt that obsolete attitudes to sex should be put aside, but on the other hand it should not be forgotten that sex also performs a sociopolitical function which cannot be ignored. Without entering into details, suffice it to say that what is often presented as progress is merely a disguised form of regression which is sociobiologically and politically unacceptable. Curiously enough that progress is often proclaimed in capitalist countries by professionals who declare themselves to be socialists or Marxists. This so-called sexual freedom explains the expanding of commercialized pornography, the growing number of 'sex shops' and the increase of sexual abuse, particularly of children.

Criminologically, the formulation of special types of offence and corresponding classification belong to the past. Close scrutiny of what was said at the meetings mentioned above will show that the mentally abnormal, sexual and habitual offenders were not considered as types in the strict sense of the term but as something presenting an ensemble of features which were also present in other descriptions of offenders. In sum, the term 'types' was understood as having a relative character. Yet some useful guidelines for the treatment of the offenders involved were formulated.

The situation is different concerning recidivists. If this is understood to mean relapse into crime, whether or not the offences have been detected, one may ask whether recidivism is not the most common feature among offenders. In other words, the primary offender is more a legal fiction than a sociopolitical reality. As for the young adult offender, fortunately his image has been gradually fading, partly because the conservative criminology that created it has practically disappeared, and partly because in contemporary post-industrial society the role played by young adults differs considerably from that assigned to them in the industrial society and demands a greater share of social responsibility.

Non-institutional treatment

From the beginning non-institutional treatment has been a constant feature of United Nations criminal policy. In the 1950s preference was given to probation and related measures while in the 1970s community-based forms of treatment came to the fore. In either case, Western conceptions were and are influential and often accepted without taking into account that the clientele of such treatment is no longer what it was when non-institutional measures were advocated, and that the term 'community' is often used in a figurative sense which in many cases does not correspond to reality, particularly to urban reality in the vast majority of countries.

In 1951 the study *Probation and Related Measures* was prepared by the Secretariat with the cooperation of the ILO, UNESCO, WHO, the Howard League for Penal Reform, IPPC, and such eminent professionals as Barnett, Christiansen, Clerc, Cornil, Kadecka and Sellin. It was followed by *Practical Results and Financial Aspects of Adult Probation in Selected Countries,* 1954, prepared by Max Grünhut, Reader in Criminology at the University of Oxford.[6]

The aim of the 1951 study was to set up a series of definitions badly needed in view of the existing confusion, to offer some information about the origin of the measures involved and their development, to produce some useful data and to submit some practical conclusions. Most of the data was taken from the USA, United Kingdom, New Zealand, Norway, Sweden and the Netherlands.

Summarily stated, the conclusions were that probation is a method of dealing with specially selected offenders, and it means the conditional suspension of punishment by placing the offender under personal supervision and giving guidance or treatment. It deals with offenders whose guilt has been established, but in some countries the method has been extended to persons who are not regarded as offenders because they are juveniles. The 'suspension of punishment' may mean either suspension of the criminal proceedings or passing a sentence but suspending its execution.

Although, historically, probation has been developed as an alternative to imprisonment, it may be employed as an alternative to any kind of punishment and therefore its use should not be restricted to a particular kind of offence. Probation means a period during which the probationer is expected to comply with certain conditions, the non-fulfilment of which usually, although not always, implies the revocation of the benefit.

Probation does not mean leniency or a let-off, but treating offenders in a way which does not imply imprisonment. Therefore, any abuse or misuse of probation will discredit the concept, which in any case should not be identified with pardon or commutation. It is a misconception to think it may be applied only to young or first offenders. The absence of criminal record is desirable but by itself should not preclude probation.

As related measures, parole, which is a conditional release, and recognizance or binding over were examined, as well as the suspension of the execution of the sentence already in practice in some countries which, as a rule, does not imply supervision or assistance.

The second study was undertaken following the recommendation made by the 1950 ad hoc group of experts which was confirmed in the following year by the Social Commission. The conclusions were that probation is recognized as a successful measure for the rehabilitation of offenders, but that two prerequisites are essential – the adequate selection of offenders, and the availability of professional staff as probation officers or equivalent. As for the rate of success or failure, consideration should be given to the corresponding penal system and the existing social conditions, which for all practical purposes means that by itself probation cannot do what the penal system prevents or makes unnecessarily difficult and social conditions do not permit. Prediction methods alone never warrant a final decision. The costs of probation are considerably below those of imprisonment, but this does not mean the probation should replace imprisonment or the latter be avoided simply for financial reasons.

Of considerable importance was the remark made by Professor Grünhut that probation was already in a transitional period which should be taken into account by countries contemplating its introduction. Nowadays, the supervision implied in probation is often resisted by probationers, particularly the young. Moreover, the growing mobility of post-industrial society makes probation more difficult and expensive, and the costs of the personnel required to make really effective not only supervision but also assistance are increasing in every country. In sum, although still having a good non-institutional value, probation cannot fulfil the role it did in the industrial society in which it was born.

In accordance with resolutions adopted by the Social Commission and ECOSOC in 1949 and 1950 respectively, Professor C.Th. Kempe's study *Parole and After-Care,* (Criminological Institute, Utrecht, 1954) examines the basic principles of parole, definition, content, aims, the role of the judiciary, nature and scope of after-care, organization and the results obtained in a group of selected countries, not only European. The main conclusions were the obvious usefulness of parole if properly organized, and if followed when necessary and possible by adequate after-care which may be extended in some cases to the parolee's family; that the kinds of parole vary all over the world; that in some countries in spite of the advantages of parole there is little or no interest in introducing it; that to be effective parole requires a thorough preparation period, which is often neglected, and a careful selection of parolees which is not always carried out as it should be; that in some countries only penitentiary authorities deal with parole, ignoring the view that lay participation should not be dispensed with or reduced to a mere formality since it would be unrealistic to put parole only in the hands of professional people, that is to say, parole and after-care should be regarded as a joint activity; parole may be granted more than once to the same person; and greater criminological research is required in order to make parole and after-care more effective.

At the Second Congress in 1960, the subject of pre-release treatment and after-care as well as assistance to dependents of prisoners was fully discussed. The recommendations were: that pre-release treatment is an integral part of the process of justice; that in pre-release treatment due attention should be paid to the specific problems inherent in the transition from institutional life to life in the community; that permission to work outside the prison should be granted as much as possible as part of the pre-release period; that the releasing authority should have some discretion, within the framework of legal regulations, in granting and organizing the pre-release and after-care; that the main purpose of after-care is to bring about as effectively as possible the reintegration of the offender into the life of the free community and to give him or her moral and material aid; that since after-care is part of the rehabilitation process it should be made available to all persons released from prison; that the cooperation of private agencies must be sought, as well as the cooperation of the public which can be facilitated by the use of all information media; that special attention should be given to the after-care of the handicapped, abnormal offenders, alcoholics, drug addicts and dependents; that dependents should not be made to suffer by reason of the offender's imprisonment, and therefore satisfactory relations with the family and with other persons should be encouraged as much as possible; and that the advisability of allowing conjugal visits should be carefully studied.

Although some of the recommendations are behind some contemporary pre-release programmes and practices, particularly concerning conjugal visits, most of them may be regarded as constituting a sort of manual of obvious practical value. One of the greatest contributions is that nothing should be organized on the purely routine administrative basis still unfortunately extremely frequent in many countries. The participation of the community, at present so much proclaimed, was already stressed and regarded as a vital piece of the whole institution.

At the Third Congress, in 1965, probation and other non-institutional measures were fully discussed and the main points made were that probation is a very flexible form of treatment; that in the selection of probationers the sentencing authority should be guided by a pre-sentencing investigation; that since probation is a form of treatment in the community it requires the acceptance and support of the public; that probation is one of the least costly and most effective ways of combating criminality; that there are sufficient data to warrant the conclusion that probation reduces recidivism; that the probation system cannot simply be transplanted to cultural settings different from those where it was devised; and that group counselling methods have proved particularly useful with hostile and aggressive probationers.

At the Fourth Congress, in 1970, probation and after-care were again examined when participation of the public in the prevention and control of crime and delinquency was discussed. Again it was stated that probation should combine the work of professionals and of volunteers, that community groups should be organized and become an integral part of both probation and after-care, and that in the organization of such groups the cooperation of young people and of ex-offenders should be enlisted as much as possible.

In the summing up of the work done by the Congress, Sir Leon Radzinowicz stated that public participation could not be assumed to be good in all circumstances, nor could it be rejected altogether, therefore gradations should be made. He added that all should be subject at intervals to scientific and detailed re-evaluation. His main conclusion was that public participation could never be a major instrument of crime control. Nevertheless public participation has already played and will continue to play a fruitful and socially inspiring role. His apt remarks deserve full attention particularly from those who since then have advocated community participation in a rather theoretical way.

At the Fifth Congress, in 1975, under the item 'treatment of offenders in custody or in the community, with special reference to the implementation of the Standard Minimum Rules' the alternatives to imprisonment were discussed. It was pointed out that in many countries the role and functions of penal institutions were the subject of vigorous debate, and there was a crisis of confidence regarding the effectiveness of imprisonment. Further, it was argued that in some instances the experience of imprisonment was so harmful as seriously to impair the ability of the offender to resume a law-abiding existence upon being released. Other participants urged that caution be exercised in order to avoid overemphasizing the negative aspects of imprisonment, and expressed confidence that some closed institutions had demonstrated their effectiveness in re-educating and resocializing offenders to some extent. There was none the less a substantial consensus that the use of imprisonment should be restricted to those offenders who needed to be neutralized in the interest of public safety and for the protection of society.

Treatment programmes within a community involved important problems both for the penal administrator and the community concerned. First among these was that of locating within the community areas and facilities suitable for schemes of that nature, with a view to treatment being given within the community from which the offender had come or remained while serving his sentence or to which he would return after serving his sentence. Secondly, it was necessary for the community to accept some form of direct or indirect responsibility in the treatment process. Furthermore, a wide range of supportive services to assist supervision was necessary.

Two aspects relating to the use of community treatment schemes, the unique feature of which was to put the offender in a position of helping others instead of being an object of help, were referred to as being of significance. Firstly, the promulgation of laws and enactments without adequate resources for implementing them might tend to make any attempt to carry out alternative treatment measures futile. Secondly, the development of advisory and technical services to assist the courts or administrative organs responsible for making decisions as to the categories and individuals suitable for such treatment should not be overlooked.

The need for a wider use of non-institutional treatment was again put forward at the Sixth Congress, in 1980, during discussion of the item 'deinstitutionalization of corrections and its implications for the residual prisoner', on which the Secretariat submitted a working paper which is excellent in many respects but may be criticized in others.[7] The use of the term 'corrections' is unfortunate since it reflects an approach which belongs to the past. The same may be said about 'deinstitutionalization' and 'residual'. By using the former it is overlooked that even non-institutional treatment often requires the frequent or constant intervention of several types of institution. The identification of 'prison' with 'institution' has led to an obvious conceptual confusion which should be avoided. The justification of penal institutions, which can be of many kinds, is determined by the extent of the protection required. As for 'residual', suffice it to repeat that even if the term refers only to long-term prisoners, they should not be regarded as a residuum, that is, as something left over.

On the positive side the Secretariat's paper clearly points out the necessity of improving conditions practically everywhere, and the need for alternative measures at all levels of the criminal justice system, which confirms how difficult it would be to dispense with institutional functions. The remarks made by the Secretariat about community service and corrective labour deserve full attention, provided that account is taken of the difficulties involved, and that as already stated in quite a number of cases the community cannot provide what is asked from it as long as crime, particularly official, political, ideological and economic crime, is not considerably reduced. As for corrective labour, some of the remarks made, as well as many past and present data concerning a number of countries, show that in most cases it is more inhuman and cruel than institutional treatment.

The main conclusion is that as long as treatment, whether institutional or not, is maintained under the obsolete flag of correction much of the criticism addressed to institutional treatment applies also to non-institutional treatment. The criticism would be considerably reduced if the SMR were applied as they should be in all countries.

The assertion that the 'process of stigmatization and marginalization starts at the very earliest stage of the criminal process' cannot be taken seriously, however much support is given to it by 'progressive' professionals. No doubt in some cases stigmatization and marginalization occur, but generalizations of this type should be avoided. There are everywhere enough data to show that many offenders who never 'enter' into the penal process are already stigmatized or marginalized by a variety of factors. Others, if stigmatized for penal reasons, are certainly not marginalized and regard themselves and are regarded as respectable and play important or significant roles in society. This is particularly the case with many political, ideological or financially-minded offenders.

What should be kept in mind is that in the same way as the industrial society of the past created its own conception and machinery of treatment, so the post-industrial society of our time is expected to create its own. The task is certainly not easy. Actually the persistent use of 'progressive' generalizations aiming at the abolition of prison, the so-called legalization of the use of narcotic drugs and the acceptance of a variety of forms of deviance, so often put forward in some capitalist countries, give the impression of being a cover to evade the difficulties involved in a sociopolitical construction of the criminal policy required by our time and the immediate future.

As possible tenets for the treatment of offenders in contemporary society the following are suggested: more effective security and protection of the community at the national and international levels; greater use of science and technology in the treatment and control of offenders; the organization of penal systems on a systemic and cost-analysis basis; and all three of the above to be set within the framework of a real preservation of individual and collective human rights.

This is not the place to evolve the particulars of each tenet but suffice it to say that the present distinction between institutional and non-institutional treatment would be less marked than it is, and that according to the principle of eligibility, which should be understood sociopolitically, the primary beneficiaries of the treatment of offenders would be the non-offender and society. This does not mean a regression to old repressive conceptions, but the formulation of a type of treatment in which prevention and protection are of the essence. The reference already made to human rights means that the return to old repressive conceptions is not advocated. Among other things the traditional aims of rehabilitation, readaptation, resocialization, re-education, reinsertion and the like so often favoured for professional interests will be remodelled and become part of the security and protection mentioned.

It may be argued that the approach suggested will never be accepted as part of United Nations criminal policy. In rebuttal, only a few years ago the same was said about crime and the abuse of power, with reference to offences and offenders beyond the reach of the law, which, with all its implications, is nowadays one of the most prominent items of that policy. The same may be said about the consideration of victims and some aspects of criminal justice, some of which have already been discussed. In fact, the inclusion of these items in the 1970s clearly shows the great sense of responsibility of the Secretariat with respect to the Purposes and Principles of the Charter of which, criminal policy is part. Needless to say that sense of responsibility was matched by that of the General Assembly, the Economic and Social Council and the Committee on Crime Prevention and Control.

Development and planning

As part of the general overview (see chapter 1) documentary references have been made to development and planning in connection with criminal policy matters. Within reasonable limits owing to the large amount of documents dealing directly with both subjects, so closely related to the crime problem, what follows offers some guidance in the complex relationship between crime, development and planning.

The use of both concepts as basic components of criminal policy has been the result of a long policy-making process. At the end of the nineteenth century development and planning were often sensed and sometimes specifically used, particularly but not only by criminologists coming from what at that time was called scientific socialism. By referring to poverty, social injustice, poor or miserable living conditions, lower classes and the need for a different socioeconomic structure, even conservative criminologists were aware of the meaning of development if not of planning. Later, under colonialism 'development' became a commonplace term used to denote the inability of a country or territory to expand economically and therefore in need of economic aid to overcome the condition of underdevelopment. As for planning, the concept was already used, often for theoretical purposes, by some French and English economists, and criticized by Engels who accused them of not following Marx in the interpretation of the term.[8] No doubt others also used the terms plan, planned and planning when dealing with socioeconomic structures, social change and the like.

Concerning United Nations criminal policy, already at the 1948 and 1950 meetings of the ad hoc committee of experts questions affecting development and crime were discussed, and the need for advance planning clearly stated. At that time the Secretariat was fully aware that the expansion of UN membership, mostly as a result of the decolonization process, required the consideration of the crime problem from an angle very different from that of the Western countries. Briefly, instead of looking for causal theories, the approach was to regard crime in close connection with development. The approach was initiated in the *Programme of Concerted Practical Action in the Social Field* (E/CN.5/291,1953). It was at the 1953 meeting of the ad hoc committee of experts that the Secretariat suggested that the question of the prevention of types of crime resulting from social changes and accompanying economic development in less developed countries should be one of the items to be discussed at the coming Congress, which was to be the first one. The question was, however, regarded as complex and demanding more detailed examination. Moreover, owing to historical factors already described, preference was given to treatment matters. Nevertheless, it was said that the subject constituted the most important foundation for the planning of criminal policy. Further, it was suggested that field investigations should be undertaken with the cooperation of local research bodies. As part of the new approach the correlation between development and crime was also discussed at seminars or regional social defence meetings: it was one of the factors that prompted the suggestion already mentioned asking for the organization of regional institutes.

At the Second Congress, in 1960, two general reports were submitted on the *Prevention of Types of Criminality Resulting from Social Changes and Accompanying Economic Development in Less Developed Countries* (A/CONF.17/3 and 4), one prepared by J.J. Panakal, of India and A.M. Khalifa, of Egypt, as UN consultants, and the other by the Secretariat. In both the relationship between socioeconomic developments and prevention of crime was considered on the basis of available data on demographic, environmental, economic, cultural, town planning, industrialization, migration and other components of social change and development. More specifically, the second report stressed that the purpose was to set up the basis of a criminal policy by connecting, through rational planning, social policy and the problem of crime. It was stated that as a rule social breakdown precedes the creation of new social codes or values, that orderly social change is not easy, and that serious national and international efforts were needed to understand the relationship between social change and criminality; also that policy planners should pay attention to the development of a sound social policy realistically designed to prevent crime.

The summary records of the Second Congress clearly show that discussions on the subject were not confined to what were then called less developed countries. It was pointed out that lack of security may be regarded as the result of how development was understood and carried out. While some stressed the preventive function of economic improvement others, without rejecting it, argued that the way in which that improvement takes place sometimes leads to the growth of crime. The conclusion was that economic development has an ambivalent function, and that its ambivalence was the result of the complexity of the development process in which other non-economic factors operate.

The term 'less developed countries' was considered disparaging and eventually rejected. The reasoning was that the process of development shows that the use of very advanced techniques may coexist with very little development in other fields, and that actually all countries were developing countries. It was agreed that, if used, the term 'less developed' should apply only to the economic field.

The recommendations adopted mention a variety of factors which, in different degrees, may be present in any development process. From the operational point of view it was said that social change is subject to a certain degree of control and should be a matter of national planning; that the prevention of criminality should be coordinated, if possible by an agency organized for this purpose, and constituted by highly qualified persons; and that such an agency should operate as an integral part of a coordinated scheme for national, social and economic planning. The United Nations as well as the institutes should undertake studies on the correlation of crime, development and planning.

At the Third Congress, in 1965, the issues of social change and criminality, and social forces and the prevention of crime, closely related to the crime–development–planning trilogy, were discussed, but since, unfortunately, contrary to its purpose the Congress did not adopt any resolution or recommendation, only references to some of the remarks having some weight in development and planning matters can be made here. Among them were those concerning the importance of changes of attitude among juveniles and young people; the depersonalization caused by uncontrolled urbanization (which was somewhat contradicted by those who asserted that greater individualization was one of the characteristics of some contemporary societies); the excessive preoccupation with economic development; and the role of migration. Other references may be found in the lectures given by B.K. Bhattacharya, of India, and H. Kefacha, of Tunisia on 'Approaches to Crime Prevention in Rapidly Changing Societies' and 'Youth and Criminality in Africa' respectively. In both the ambivalent character of social change was pointed out, also the transformation of old institutions, the increasing process of disintegration caused by urbanization, the growing lack of employment opportunities, and the breakdown of family groups in developing countries.

As previously stated, issue no. 25 of the *International Review of Criminal Policy* (1967), was devoted to development and planning (see chapter 1). Suffice it to say here that perhaps in some papers the importance of economic development was stressed without at the same time making the necessary sociopolitical reservations. The assertion that the essence of social planning is the launching of activities for continuing integration, made by Carney in his contribution, needs specifications which are not given. Of more practical character was the assertion that cost analysis problems play a significant role in development, planning and crime, made by Wilson in his excellent contribution; and the news, announced by Grygier, that already in Canada the position of director of correctional planning had been created.

More specifically the correlation between crime, development and planning was discussed at the Fourth Congress, in 1970, under the item 'Social Defence policies in relation to development planning'. This had as a basis the working papers prepared by the Secretariat and WHO, and the reports of the 1969 ad hoc group of experts and of the regional preparatory meetings for the Congress. At the discussions it was said that crime, prevention and development had a multi-significant character which does not always facilitate the understanding of such concepts; that the main question for the planner was how to deal effectively with the various aspects of development so as to achieve economic growth and higher levels of living, while at the same time preventing crime and delinquency; and that planning also demands the review and reform of criminal law and of the legal system and the availability of data which are as accurate as possible. It was also said that the problems involved in development, planning and crime extend beyond national boundaries, and that research and technical help were needed to achieve the required development and planning if crime was to be effectively prevented.

The conclusion that social defence planning should be an integral part of national planning was challenged by some participants, among them the author, who stated that this should not be understood in absolute terms since social defence problems are outside such integration. More to the point was the conclusion stressing, as had been done at the previous Congress, that effective planning demands reliable and comprehensive statistical data – which unfortunately do not exist in many countries, or if they do are quite often not made available for political or other reasons. In his excellent summing up, Sir Leon Radzinowicz specifically referred to the recognition made by the meeting of Experts on Social Policy and Social Planning, in Stockholm in 1969, that economic development is only an aspect of social development, thus opposing the thesis of integration stating that it would mean the disappearance of social defence. Moreover, Sir Leon said, integration might give the public the dangerous impression that dealing with crime called for no more than a form of social service. He also suggested that the United Nations could produce and keep up to date a small manual on social change, social planning and social defence.

In 1975 the Department of Economic and Social Affairs published the study *Popular Participation in Decision-making for Development* to which very little attention has been paid by those interested in criminal policy planning. The study shows that community participation in every field raises questions which up to now have remained practically untouched by those advocating community participation in criminal justice. The main points made are that popular participation in the different components of development and planning implies the previous consideration of the kinds of such participation, and the nature and permanence of the opportunities offered; that decisions must be made often taking into account the role of the administrators of certain services; and that consideration should be given to the cost involved. In other words, the study tries to convey the view that community participation, so often advocated (and not only in the criminal policy field), should not be improvised as often happens. In fact, the analysis of some of the failures of community participation shows that in organizing it very little attention has been paid to the complexity of development and that of the community itself. As the study states, popular participation on a sustained and efficient basis rarely emerges spontaneously. More often than not, mobilization and constant support are needed, including guidance and supervision.

At the Fifth Congress, 1975, the item 'Economic and Social Consequences of Crime: New Challenges for Research and Planning' offered a good opportunity to remind governments of something repeatedly suggested but put aside by them. Certainly governments are not compelled to accept what is submitted for their consideration, but on the other hand the signs that they really consider what is recommended to them already exist. The need for cost analysis thinking in criminal justice questions was reasserted; its planners should not dispense with it; development of indigenous criminal justice research was necessary before suggesting anything, and the special nature of national and criminal policy planning should always be kept in mind. It is important to note that the Congress drew attention to something generally overlooked – that whatever the quality of socioeconomic planning, official action and negligence may provoke the crime that the planning tries to prevent. The suggestion was that effective control measures should be geared to changes in official actions as well as individual behaviour. The remark has an evident practical value which should not be ignored by those dealing with development, planning and criminal justice.

The Caracas Declaration adopted at the Sixth Congress in 1980 refers to development and planning when it states that the prevention of crime and criminal justice should be considered in the context of economic development, political systems, social and cultural values and social change as well as in that of the new international economic order. With respect to planning, the Declaration insists on what has already been said, that is, it demands effective capacity for its formulation.

The Congress also recommended that greater dissemination of legal knowledge through the school, university, educational and cultural institutions and public organizations is needed. As far as development, planning and criminal policy are concerned this recommendation has a significance which, if properly implemented under real democratic regimes, will contribute to a more effective development and crime prevention and at the same time facilitate community participation in criminal justice matters.

Mention should be made here of the *Report of the Working Group of Experts from Latin America and the Caribbean on Criminal Policy and Development* (A/CONF.87/BP/7,1980) which, although related to the Caracas Congress, constitutes by itself a significant contribution to the understanding of the relationship between development, planning and crime. In its conclusions the Group stated that national development planning should include criminal policy experts; that each country should establish a criminal policy body which, in addition to its national functions, would be responsible for ensuring international cooperation; and that the relationship between development and crime also implies a twofold process of criminalization and decriminalization – the first concerning, among others, – activities directed against national wealth such as ecological protection, traffic in persons and drugs, and the second the decriminalization of crimes currently having little social importance. The last recommendation has the merit of being probably the first to refer to the process of criminalization and decriminalization as part of development.

Another aspect seldom mentioned when discussing the correlation here considered is the interdependence between development, armaments and crime. In this respect the data, remarks and conclusions of the *Study on the Relationship between Disarmament and Development* (A/36/356,1981), prepared by the Secretary-General, offer a panorama that has not yet been explored by criminal policy professionals and barely at the international level. The analysis of this long and praiseworthy report demonstrates how the expanding arms race and the expenses involved in it, whatever the extent of the manpower used in producing armaments, seriously affect the development of every country, and more particularly of the developing ones which for a variety of reasons participate in that race. If, as repeatedly stated, development and crime are deeply interlocked, then logically armaments expenses, when beyond reasonable limits, contribute effectively to the increase of a variety of crimes among which some forms of economic crime and criminal corruption should not be overlooked. According to the data mentioned and the observations made in the report, there is an evident link between development, the armaments race and criminality or, put in another way, the reasonable reduction of armaments expenses would facilitate the prevention of a variety of criminal offences perpetrated by the elevated, the underprivileged, and those in between. Among other assertions and data the following are extremely significant: there is a manifest relationship between greater development and the reduction of armaments, while on the average these expenses have been increasing in the last twenty years. According to the *World Development Report, 1980,* 570 million people are undernourished, 300 million are illiterate, 1,500 million have little or no access to medical services, and 250 million children do not go to school, yet in the past 30 years states have collectively allocated 5–8 per cent of the world's disposable resources to armaments. Moreover, given that world military expenditure in 1980 was an even $500,000 million, the global arms bill in the year 2000 is expected to be of the order of $940,000 million at 1980 prices.

The analysis of these and other data when compared with the way in which criminal justice is 'administered' in most countries, and the prevailing social condition of the clientele of the 'administration' as well as the extent of crime (see below under this heading) shows that the so-called 'military security' considerably impairs the general feeling of security in the majority of countries, with all the repercussions that its weakening implies so far as some types of crimes are concerned. It also shows that expanding military power seriously affects the sense of freedom, and of individual and collective security, with similar implications, particularly when armament competition is going on; that economic growth cannot be achieved or is notoriously below what it should be; and that as long as armament expenses expand, the gap between the different social groups will be widened, particularly in developing countries. The proclaimed need for a new international economic order, industrialization and other fundamental aims of development are also seriously affected, and with them the prevention of crime, compensation of its victims, the treatment of offenders and the badly needed renewal of the vast majority of penal systems. It should be added that in many cases the arms race is accelerated by the existence of dictatorial regimes of every sort in which the military often play the primary role.

As an example of the above analysis, it can be said that in the 31 least developed countries listed in document A.1982/Add.1/Rev.1 (1982), the relationship between the conditions of development, military expenses, crime – not only common crime – and the functioning of criminal justice confirms that the armaments race is an important factor. Some governments will reply that the armaments question is a domestic matter outside international action. This reasoning is contradicted by several General Assembly resolutions asking governments to reduce arms expenses for the benefit of peace and development. To avoid any misunderstanding I should say that armaments are needed within the limits of human rights among which, as we will see, the right to development is of primary importance.

Since this is not the moment to pursue other aspects of the analysis initiated by the author, suffice it to say that the question arises as to whether, in dealing with development and crime, the armaments race should not be regarded as a serious conditioning factor.

The *Report of the Working Group of Governmental Experts on the Right to Development* (E/CN.4/1489,1982) confirms that the right to development is jeopardized when the right to live in peace (General Assembly resolution 33/73 on the Declaration on the Preparation of Societies for Life in Peace) is not only seriously threatened but actually violated. According to the report the holders of the right to development in its collective dimension are peoples and 'States' (curiously, while the report uses a capital 'S' for States it uses a small 'p' for peoples which, as already stated and according to the Charter, are far more important) and besides embracing the social, economic, cultural and other current components the right to development includes the rights of self-determination, equality of opportunity for all nations and individuals, territorial integrity, non-aggression, peaceful coexistence, non-intervention and elimination of world disparities. Further, the right to development states that development entails the duty on the part of each state to establish a dialogue and authentic cooperation. It is also recalled that 'performance of the obligation to ensure development is a condition for the legitimacy of Governments', a very sound assertion which, as far as criminal policy is concerned, raises many questions, most of them so far barely touched by national and international research and programming. Finally, as a *whole* the Group agreed that the demands of development cannot justify any derogation from fundamental rights. Apparently this was not accepted by some of the governmental representatives, including some from undemocratic regimes. Once again the analysis of the way in which development is carried out in some developing countries run by dictatorial regimes of a military character confirms that the development and criminality correlation is stronger than ever.

Development and crime are also closely related when the first is based on racial discrimination policies, particularly apartheid, which the 1973 Convention for its suppression and punishment defines as a crime. Here again the *Report of the Economic and Social Council* (A/37/3,1982) offers, not only on this specific matter, sufficient foundations to conclude that many forms of serious crime, particularly those committed from above, are closely related to the way in which development is carried out.

In February 1983 the Commission on Human Rights discussed the right to development on the basis partly of the report of government experts mentioned above and partly of other documents. References were made to the new international economic order (some of the references were of a purely ideological and rhetorical character); to the need to strengthen popular participation in the development process; to the status of the 1966 Covenants on Human Rights; and to capital punishment and popular participation. Of particular significance was the statement made by the Assistant Secretary-General for Human Rights, K. Herndl, that freedom from fear and freedom from want can only be achieved if conditions are created whereby everyone may really enjoy his economic, social, cultural, civil and political rights. The representative of the International Commission of Jurists stressed the fact that particularly in the South Asian region the exploitation of workers, women and children had not only continued but had intensified. Again the interdependence of development and crime is undeniable.[9]

The conclusions adopted in 1981 at the International Conference on Development, Human Rights and the Rule of Law, organized by the International Commission of Jurists at The Hague, make an important contribution to a better understanding of what development means. It was stated that development is a global concept which includes civil, political, economic, social and cultural rights; that true development implies that all human rights are inseparable and should be respected and that the right to development means far more than economic aims; also that militarism is the negation of development and people should evolve their own participation procedures so as to make really effective the decisions taken on development.

The exposition above shows the gradual evolution of the concept of development; that in that evolution there is a certain amount of repetition, which partly has been reflected here; that although the term 'planning' is frequently used there is no clear concept of it; and that the way in which development is planned and carried out in many countries is frequently a source of crime. Does all this mean that criminal development has become a new kind of crime? In view of what has already been said about new kinds of crime the answer is in the negative. Unfortunately 'penal systems' and many professionals are inclined to justify new criminalizations, i.e. to create new types of criminal offence which in turn will justify more judges and special courts, new criminal procedures and above all a lack of criminal justice. This will be referred to later when dealing with the subject of criminal justice.

More and more frequently the term 'planning' is used at the international level, not only concerning criminal policy; suffice it to say here that 'planning', 'plan', 'reform' and 'programme' are often used indiscriminately. 'Reform' can be the negation of something planned: it can also be an attempt to correct the malfunctioning of something already operating. Reforms may be part of a plan, but quite often are not, and by themselves do not constitute real planning. 'Programme' is a term very much in use particularly to justify theories, inquiries or simply professional aims. They are not often justified. The whole history of rehabilitation is full of programmes which have yielded scanty results. (Admittedly financial resources have often been lacking, and this has sometimes prevented the putting into effect of a programme scientifically correct but sociopolitically unjustified.) Both capitalist and non-capitalist countries are extremely fond of 'planning' but seldom seem to plan the administration of justice. As far as the author knows although the term 'penal *system*' is often used, very few countries have one. What the vast majority have is a variety of criminal justice services or agencies under different ministries, often competing with one another.

'Planning' means first an ensemble of efforts deliberately undertaken in accordance with some sociopolitical aims, using scientific and technical premises and carried out by a plurality of services, agencies and professionals in a coordinated way; secondly, it means the correlation of what is going to be done with what is done at other levels dealing with fundamental policies; thirdly, it means having a clear idea of what a system is and how criminal justice should be organized by structuring the main aims in the corresponding subsystems of the system; and finally, it means that in all this process the community should actively participate. Consequently 'criminal justice planning' means the ensemble of undertakings deliberately pursued by a diversity of agencies and the community, aiming at the formulation and functioning of a penal system within the context of the main national development policies.

The New International Economic Order

The NIEO has become an essential ingredient in any discussion concerning development and the right to it. The expression is not new; it was already in use in 1945, but it was only later, when the 'decades of development' were postulated, that the NIEO became an essential element in practically every discussion and was brought into criminal policy.

The field embraced by the NIEO is enormous; sometimes it is enlarged or reduced in accordance with ideological approaches, the main poles of which are capitalism and marxism. The subjects usually referred to are commodity problems, national resources, producers' associations, price increases, transnational activities and usages, income stabilization, food security and trade, recovery, change, tariff barriers, restrictive business practices, technological activities, new horizons in trade cooperation, supporting mechanisms and many others of which only a few are directly related to certain kinds of crime.

The references made at the 1978 session of the CCPC to the NIEO and the problem of crime were incidental and ideologically inspired, as was the case with the reference made by the Caracas Declaration in 1980. The correct assertion that, in order to clarify the references to the NIEO and the problem of crime, the CCPC should establish closer links with the bodies concerned with social development was resisted by the representatives of several countries, among which some socialist countries were persistent (*Social Development Questions*, E/1981/3). On the other hand, the links were stressed again by the General Assembly (A/36/645,1981) but ignored by the report of ECOSOC (A/37/3,1982).

The analysis of *Studies on the Effects of the Operations of Transnational Corporations: Review of Ongoing and Future Research* (E/CN. 10/1983/13) makes no useful reference to the links so often referred to in a rather vague way. The most recent *Study on the New International Economic Order and the Promotion of Human Rights* (E/CN.4/ Sub.2/1983/24) deals with financial resources, external debt, transnational corporations, armaments and other matters which are sometimes directly connected with crime, particularly institutional crime; but the document ignores this connection, and also the fact that no development and effective promotion of human rights will ever take place as long as dictatorial regimes proliferate which, beside denying every human right, prevent the community from participating actively in national development. As the study states, 'the poor countries are like ships in distress', but there is no doubt that the distress will continue and get worse as long as the 'ships' are under the captaincy of dictatorial regimes. The claims against colonialism, imperialism and the like are justified, but one may ask what the protesting countries were doing before imperialism started, that is when they were independent nations or groups centuries ago.

The Charter of Economic Rights and Duties of States, 1974, offers some foundations to establish the links so often mentioned, but little progress will be made as long as sovereignty and the rights to financial and natural resources (the latter are the only ones mentioned by the Charter) are not subordinated to the effectiveness of the principles and purposes of the United Nations Charter. In other words, the ideological manoeuvring of obsolete concepts and at the same time advocating a NIEO without realizing that the latter requires the almost radical transformation of those concepts will yield numerous reports but scanty practical results.

Certainly the NIEO and NINCJO are linked in many respects, but their meaning requires clarification which for the former is still missing, and for the latter is only now being initiated. In any case, the NIEO cannot be understood in purely economic terms. This assertion may be objected to by stating that 'economic order' means what it says, that is, the pursuance of a new economic structure which is needed, but no economic order can be achieved without consideration for human rights. In other words the term 'order' embraces far more than the specific subject; therefore the first thing to do is to keep in mind that the formulation of a NIEO, and for that matter of a NINCJO, is a sociopolitical task, and that economic and criminal justice matters as part of United Nations aims must be formulated in accordance with the principles and purposes of the Charter and not according to those of a particular ideology.[10]

In January 1983 a Group of Experts was convened at Syracuse, Italy, by the Secretariat to deal with the connexion between the NIEO and NINCJO. On the basis of the conclusions adopted the Secretariat drafted the *Guiding Principles for Crime Prevention and Criminal Justice in the Context of Development and a New International Economic Order* as an annex to the *Discussion Guide for the Regional and Interregional Preparatory Meetings for the Seventh United Nations Congress on the Prevention of Crime and the Treatment of Offenders* (A/CONF.121/PM.1,April 1983). The attempt is encouraging for the final formulation of the bases of a NINCJO. For the final version of the *Guiding Principles* the report of the 1984 session of the CCPC

(E/1984/16) should be consulted. Of particular significance is the reference to the responsiveness of the criminal justice system to development and human rights. If account is taken of the fact that criminal justice is regarded as a system one may ask if the expression *systematic approach* should not be replaced by *systemic approach*.

The extent of crime

The expression 'extent of crime' has two meanings: one refers to the number of acts which, through a criminalization process, are legally declared as criminal offences; and the other to the number of these committed in a given period and country. Both aspects are closely related, and have been taken into account by the United Nations.

Criminalization is a sociopolitical process by which the constitutionally entrusted powers determine what kind of conduct should be regarded as criminal, and how it should be categorized. Decriminalization and depenalization are part of the same constitutional process acting in reverse. Under dictatorial regimes and more specifically under their frequently imposed 'states of emergency', criminalization is often arbitrary and constitutes a criminal abuse of power under 'legal' cover. Suffice it to say that according to the *Study of Recent Developments Concerning the Situations Known as States of Siege or Emergency* (E/CN.4/Sub.2/1982/15) the fact of 'having talked about human rights', 'tried to denounce the violation of human rights', and so on, is criminalized in some countries and severely punished.[11]

Genocide, torture, cruel, inhuman or degrading treatment or punishment, illegal arrest, hijacking, hostages, terrorism and economic crimes have been criminalized in many countries following UN directives or in accordance with international conventions, but in many of them the perpetration of these and related crimes by civil and military institutions is frequent and immune from prosecution.

'Extent of crime' is generally understood as the number of criminal offences committed in a given country and period. As a rule police statistics reflect it better than any others, but even if all statistics were reliable they would still not reveal the real extent of crime. In spite of this limitation the idea of comparing national criminal statistics so as to obtain a world-wide view of the extent of crime was already raised by F. Zahn in his paper *Internationale Kulturstatistik* submitted at the sixteenth session of the International Statistical Institute held in Rome in 1925. To Zahn the easiest way was to compare judicial statistics since, in spite of some differences, they present greater uniformity as far as serious crimes are concerned. At the next meeting of the Institute, in Cairo in 1927–8, Dr J.R.B. Roos submitted a very original paper called *Consonnes et voyelles* in which he expressed his scepticism about the possibility of comparing national criminal statistics, owing mostly to the diversity of criminal laws. On the other hand, he stated that the comparison of criminal trends was feasible. Following his suggestion a Committee was appointed which submitted a report to the eighteenth session of the Institute, in Warsaw in 1929, in which, after stressing the need for caution, the feasibility of international comparisons was admitted and, contrary to the previous view, the use of police statistics was recommended. Other experts, among them W.A. Bonger and E Roesner, concurred and the idea was accepted. A Commission was appointed with the cooperation of the International Penal and Penitentiary Commission (IPPC) and at the 1937 meeting of the Institute the report *Directives pour l'élaboration des statistiques criminelles dan. les divers pays* was submitted. Among other questions the following were examined: the validity of existing criminal statistics and publications on the subject; the system of schedules to be used in the classification of offences and offenders; references to personal and other circumstantial characteristics or conditions, including recidivism; and penalties imposed. The main purpose was to work towards a gradual cooperation and integration of governmental efforts at the international and national levels. Curiously, the priority attached to police statistics was not mentioned.

In 1947 the United Nations circulated a note to various countries, the main purpose of which was to collect data and analyze the results of the existing studies with a view to ascertaining what aspects of the problem were suitable for international action, and how the action required could best be carried out.[12] The study of the answers showed that the use of categories of offence and not of individual crimes was favoured. Professor Verkko, however, rejected the category system and favoured that of particular offences such as homicide, assault, rape, disorderly conduct, gambling, drunkenness, and so on.

At the 1950 session of the ad hoc committee of experts (E/CN.5/ 231), criminal statistics were thoroughly discussed on the basis of reports submitted by the Section of Social Defence and by V. Verkko, M. Ancel, R. Beattie and The Howard League (Series E/CN.5/AC.4/ 3 to 10). The main subjects discussed were again the question of preference between 'cases' or 'persons', that is, of offences or offenders; definitions; categories versus types; regularity and reliability of criminal statistics; usefulness of the different kinds of criminal statistics; the dark figure; distinctions between persons arrested, charged, sentenced, convicted, and so on; and the diversity of police agencies in the same country. The relationship between crime and population in the form of crime indexes per 100,000 or any round figure was discouraged, particularly by Verkko who considered it misleading as long as it was not based on the consideration of other circumstances such as sex, age, population distribution and other factors. This caution has been generally ignored and nowadays such indexes are frequently misused.

The main conclusions to be drawn from all the international efforts described are that with some exceptions the existing national criminal statistics are only relatively reliable, irregularly published and generally prepared in the same country by a diversity of organs, that is to say, centralized criminal statistics are still the exception.

At the 1953 and 1955 sessions of the ad hoc committee the question of criminal statistics was again considered, and the Secretariat was requested to prepare a study on the feasibility of a system of international criminal statistics. Accordingly the report *Criminal Statistics: Standard Classification of Offences* (E/CN.5/337,1959) was prepared by the Section of Social Defence. Tentatively the offences selected were homicide, aggravated assault and robbery. The report, highly technical in many respects, reviewed the terminological difficulties involved; reporting varieties; the different ways in which schedules were prepared and used; the possibility of including other offences if the attempt succeeded; and other questions. The text was circulated among UN correspondents and to some experts, and their comments were analyzed by the Section. Some of the comments were taken into account in the drafting of the final report which was submitted to the Social Commission but, probably owing to its technical character, the Commission was not able to discuss it. The representatives of some European countries were so confused that on their proposal and by a majority it was decided that the discussion should be postponed instead of sending the report to the corresponding agencies of governments for comment. Since then, and in spite of the efforts of some representatives and the Secretariat, the subject has not been discussed, but this has not prevented many representatives from referring to criminal statistics as urgent at every possible opportunity. The last was at the Sixth Congress, in 1980, which, by its resolution no. 2, stressed the need for a world-wide reliable system of criminal statistics so as to facilitate access to the required information about the phenomenon of crime, development and the functioning of justice systems. Accordingly the Secretary-General is requested to intensify efforts to coordinate the collection of comparable national statistics on crime and justice in each of the member states and at the regional level. The same resolution recommended that all states should increase their efforts to improve information about crime.

At present the main questions involved are not technical, or even the frequent lack of criminal statistical data in many countries or the obvious lack of coordination among the organs dealing with criminal statistics; rather, the main issue is the kind of crime that the representatives had in mind when the resolution was adopted. Although the question of abuse of power was discussed at the Sixth Congress, and the existence of official, semi-official, economic, etc., offences was evident (see resolution no. 7) the fact is that the problem of criminal statistics must be considered from a different angle from that of the past, and that the attempts made to determine the extent of crime in the past were useless, whatever the technical sophistication of the questionnaires used.

In 1948 the Social Commission and ECOSOC decided that the Secretariat should prepare a report on the extent of crime. At that time crime was understood as common crime, and moreover the victims were, as we have already seen, except for some passing references, totally ignored. Although fully aware of the difficulties and of the limited results to be expected, the Section of Social Defence undertook the task and in 1950 submitted the *Statistical Report on the State of Crime* (E/CN.5/204) covering the period 1937–46. The questionnaire sent to all member states, at that time numbering about 60, referred to a large number of offences against persons, property, public health, public order, crimes against the state, treason, espionage, collaboration with the enemy, and so on. The questionnaire also asked about penalties of less than six months, from six to 12 months, from one to five years and more than five years. Thirty-seven member states replied, i.e. 60 per cent of the then membership, a record which has not since been beaten; from the Eastern European countries Poland was the only one which replied. The information provided was of varied quality and extent. The most complete was about imprisonment but statistically the effort to present a world-wide panorama of crime failed. With some exceptions the answers reflected the poverty of criminal statistics; the fact that many governments had apparently done very little to remedy the situation; and that a sizeable number of them were unwilling to provide data.[13]

In pursuance of General Assembly resolution 302(XXVII) 1972, all member states were invited to provide information concerning crime prevention and control in their respective countries. The idea was to present a world-wide analysis of the problem, including its extent, and of the administration of justice. Sixty-five answers were received, but only 50 were used owing to the faulty condition of the others. The figures received concerned intentional homicide, assault, sex crimes, kidnapping, robbery, theft, fraud, illegal drug abuse and alcohol abuse. Although technically the Secretariat submitted a good report it was extremely constrained; the report included a variety of data concerning 50 countries, many of which lacked reliable criminal statistics. From Eastern Europe only Czechoslovakia, the German Democratic Republic, Poland and Yugoslavia answered. The report presents crime rates per 100,000 population for developing and developed countries the value of which is extremely limited. The general conclusions were that crime was increasing in all the countries concerned; that political crimes were a serious problem in some countries; that criminality involving drugs was considered a dangerous threat; that terrorism was widespread; and that crimes against the environment were a serious problem mainly in developed countries. Concerning Czechoslovakia the report produced by the Academy of Sciences in 1983 showed the gravity of pollution, which apparently affects not only living conditions but also the development of the country.

Data concerning the organization of criminal justice were also presented according to rates per 100,000 population, which does not make much sense if it is remembered that by itself the population is not the only index to be considered. With respect to implementation of the Standard Minimum Rules for the Treatment of Prisoners, the report states that their influence has notably increased.

The report is interesting, but close scrutiny of the countries involved, the data included (particularly the unclear description of their sources, in spite of the frequent references to 'offences recorded'), and the general character of many of the remarks, show that the answers do not present a reasonable panorama of the extent of crime at the international level. What is quite clear is that common crime is becoming an ever more serious problem all over the world.

To common crime should be added non-conventional crime, which is constituted by that perpetrated institutionally, by ideologically or revolutionary inspired organizations or groups, by multinationals, gross negligence in the industrial, commercial and other production areas, labour exploitation, and so on. The report *Summary and Arbitrary Executions* (E/CN.4/16) 1983, submitted to the Commission on Human Rights states that the number of persons 'executed' in the last 15 years in 38 countries is not less than two million. If other UN documents dealing with 'disappearances' – usually preceded by cruel, inhuman or degrading treatment or punishment and/or torture – are taken into account, I estimate that 22 more countries should be added to those already mentioned. Resolution no. 5 of the Sixth Congress in 1980 'deplores and condemns the practice of killing and executing political opponents or suspected offenders carried out by armed forces, law enforcement or other governmental agencies or paramilitary groups or political groups' and 'affirms that such acts constitute a particularly abhorrent crime the eradication of which is a high international priority'. The Code of Conduct for Law Enforcement Officials (1979) has not prevented institutional crime by officials and members of the military from 'disposing of' and torturing people in more than 80 countries all over the world, particularly under chronic or semi-chronic 'states of emergency'. It may be argued that military forces, which include the Navy, are not law enforcement officials, which is true, but whatever their duties are they do not include executions, torture and the like. Countries under military regimes are frequently victimized by this type of criminality.

There are also war crimes, crimes against peace, mankind and security, military occupation, espionage, intelligence service activities, diplomatic abuse, illicit payments, corruption of many sorts, illicit traffic of drugs with the connivance of high civil and military officials in several countries, race riots and massacres, *sine die* police arrest or detention and criminal justice crime.

A comparative analysis of the countries internationally 'indicted' of criminally violating human rights, with the parties to the Conventions protecting those rights, shows that about 70 per cent of the 'indicted' are parties to the majority of conventions, particularly the 1966 conventions concerning social, economic, cultural, civil and political rights.[14]

As mentioned previously, the so-called penal systems also produce their own criminal victimization due to delays in criminal justice, corruption or simply by becoming docile instruments of dictatorial powers.

In sum, United Nations inquiries into the extent of crime cannot be improved by only altering the questionnaires. The one adopted, following the ad hoc meeting of experts at Rutgers University, New Jersey in 1981, besides being unnecessarily complicated is not the sole instrument to be used. Governments are the main but not the only source of information. Specialized agencies and non-government organizations may be used in accordance with the resolution adopted at the Palais de Chaillot in 1948 which was reinforced by that adopted in Geneva in 1950. To these sources of information may be added any others worthy of consideration. In any case every effort should be made to ascertain approximately the extent of world crime as one of the basic elements of UN criminal policy. The main responsibility for this does not lie with the Secretariat but with many governments whose lack of cooperation is obvious and sometimes habitual.

Juvenile delinquency

From the outset juvenile delinquency was the concern of the Temporary and Social Commissions. The main reason was that by preventing it crime would be greatly reduced; crime was then almost exclusively understood as common crime, and according to Western criminology the main ingredients of juvenile delinquency were maladjustment, unsatisfied emotional needs, deprivation of maternal care, lack of education, poor living conditions, mental health problems and any other factor affecting the lack of maturity of minors. Juvenile delinquency was an all-embracing concept covering not only the juvenile criminal but also the abandoned, neglected, uneducated, etc., minor, that is, any child 'in trouble' or in need of assistance or guidance. The fiction was completed by asserting that minors lived in a world of their own.

At the request of the Social Commission, which endorsed the recommendations made by the 1949 ad hoc committee, the Secretariat published a series of *Comparative Studies on Juvenile Delinquency* mostly devoted to the presentation of the legislation on juvenile delinquency in North America, Latin America, Asia, the Far East and the Middle East (ST/SOA/SD/1 and Add.). Australia and New Zealand appeared in issue no. 9 of the *International Review of Criminal Policy,* and information on the legislation in non-self-governing territories was published in 1953.

Even now the analysis of the legislation then published is interesting, in the sense that it shows that in spite of the efforts made the system of juvenile courts or welfare boards, particularly the former, operated effectively in the capitals or important cities but in a limited way in other areas. In some developing countries juvenile courts did not exist even if there was legislation on the matter. In countries with a relatively well-developed system of juvenile courts the operating concept of 'children in trouble' provided a clientele which, in many cases, was ignored or superficially dealt with. In countries with 'welfare boards' the situation was less unsatisfactory because, among other reasons, most of them were small countries.

At the preparatory meetings for the First Congress in 1955, particularly in those held in São Paulo, Rio de Janeiro and Rangoon, both in 1954, an attempt was made to reduce the concept of juvenile offenders by considering as such only those who have committed a criminal act, thus leaving out the vague concept of 'children in trouble' so much favoured by some leading European and American professionals. In 1954 the European Exchange Seminar on the Institutional Treatment of Juvenile Offenders (ST/TAA/Ser.C/23) was held in Vienna, and was one of the most successful seminars on the subject. Among other questions, the distinction between the different kinds of treatment and the places where they should be given received special attention, and topics carefully examined were commitment systems; types of institution; the use of penal institu-

tions in some cases; the role of observation and classification; aims
and techniques; discipline and punishment; living conditions; mental
health of the staff; and criteria of success and failure. It was stated
that the last of these may be viewed in many different ways, and
that the fact that the minor commits new offences should not necessarily be regarded as a failure of institutional treatment. The question
of the concept of juvenile delinquncy was raised, and how the distor-
tion of the concept made treatment more difficult.

The Secretariat's study, *The Prevention of Juvenile Delinquency*
– reproduced in issue no. 8 of the *International Review of Criminal
Policy* – was the basic document submitted to the First Congress
on that item.[15] The study showed the chaotic situation of the question
of age limits as one of the main criteria to determining what should
be understood by 'minor'. Countries with markedly different socioeconomic, cultural and political characteristics had adopted the same
age limit of 16 or 18 years. The difficulties in determining the causes
of juvenile delinquency in accordance with the all-embracing concept
already mentioned were pointed out, and consequently also the difficulties of effective prevention. The study advised restricting the
meaning of juvenile delinquency, and stressed the fact that juveniles
are part of the community and that any preventive policy is depen-
dent on the conciseness of what it is supposed to prevent.

The summary records of the Congress show how lively the discussion was between those in favour of maintaining the wider meaning
of delinquency and those in favour of restricting it if something
practical was to be recommended concerning prevention. It was
repeatedly stated that by advocating the restriction of the term it
was not intended that minors should be treated as adults. The battle
was won by those in favour of the inflated concept of delinquency.
The reading of the conclusions and recommendations shows the
difficulties encountered during the discussions. The usual general
references were made to the role of the community, family, school,
social services (including health services), work, and the intensification of research into the meaning of delinquency in order to
determine its causation, prediction and prevention. No reference
was made to the role of the socioeconomic and political structure
of the corresponding society, or the fact that already in some developed countries minors were playing a role which did not accord
with that of 'children in trouble'. The prevailing conviction was
that by reinforcing the family and the school and multiplying every
possible kind of social service and assistance juvenile delinquency,
including juvenile crime, would be reduced (see Report of the Congress 1956.IV.4).

At the Second Congress in London in 1960, in which some of

the new developing countries were extremely active and constructive, the question of what should be understood by juvenile delinquency was once more brought up under the item 'new forms of juvenile delinquency: their origin, prevention and treatment', for the discussion of which several reports were submitted (see Report and annexed documents mentioned in 61.IV.3). As the representative of the Secretary-General, the author again pointed out the difficulties of using an almost unlimited concept of juvenile delinquency and suggested that in order to be practical the study of its 'new' forms demanded a redefinition of what should be understood by it. It was added that as long as the unlimited term was in use the meaning of 'predelinquency' was extremely difficult to determine. The old battle was renewed, but this time it was won by those in favour of a restricted concept. The cooperation of the socialist countries, which were attending a Congress for the first time, was extremely valuable, stressing that 'juvenile delinquency cannot be considered independently from the social structure of the State' (so began the conclusion and recommendations on juvenile delinquency adopted by the Congress); it was understood that the state's socioeconomic and political structure plays a role in what should be regarded as delinquency. The expression 'new' forms, always used between quotation marks, was simply regarded as new manifestations of old forms, and not necessarily as really new styles of juvenile delinquency. Such was the case with gang activities, purposeless offences, vandalism, joy-riding and the like. Accordingly, the Congress decided that

> the problem of juvenile delinquency should not be inflated and without attempting a standard definition the term juvenile delinquency should be restricted as much as possible to violations of criminal law and that even for protection, specific offences which would penalize small irregularities or maladjusted behaviour of minors, but for which adults would not be prosecuted should not be created.

At the Third Congress in Stockholm in 1965, juvenile delinquency was not discussed, but references were made to it and its meaning as agreed at the Second Congress was regarded as the guiding one. The term 'young adult' was also under consideration, but although recognizing in such persons some specific characteristics, the creation of a special group, attempted in the past, was not raised. As is well known, the Congress did not make any kind of recommendations, therefore the concept of juvenile delinquency adopted by the previous Congress remained.[16]

At the Fourth Congress in 1970 juvenile delinquency was again not part of the agenda; it was stated that crime was a complex phenomenon involving all kinds of modalities and persons, and although the role of youth was stressed no attempt was made to go back to the inflated concept of 'children in trouble'. It should be noted that in the 1970s juvenile crime had acquired a considerable extent and gravity in some developed and developing countries. As stated, since the 1960s young persons had been taking a more significant part in society, trying to transform it in accordance with their ideas and aims. In some respects they succeeded.

At the Fifth Congress in Geneva in 1975, juvenile delinquency was not discussed either. The operating concept established by the Second Congress has settled the question, and it was obvious that the relationship between drugs, alcohol and crime raised questions which did not need to hark back to the obsolete Western concept of 'children in trouble'. The role of youth in crime in contemporary society was discussed at UNAFEI in 1978, where it was stressed that already in the 1970s young people between 14 and 21 years of age were sociopolitically active in many countries. It was to the credit of the UNAFEI seminar that the distinction between juvenile criminals and juveniles in need of assistance and care was maintained, and that the separation did not necessarily mean that juvenile offenders would be deprived of the assistance they need.[17]

Surprisingly at the Sixth Congress in 1980, under the item 'Juvenile justice: before and after the onset of delinquency' the old inflated concept of juvenile delinquency was brought back, and the traditional references to sociopsychological needs, the role of the family, school, maladjustment, etc., were offered as the main tenets of juvenile crime. According to the Branch's paper the aim of juvenile justice is to promote and safeguard the well-being of children and young people – with no reference, particularly as regards the latter, to their own responsibilities *vis-à-vis* society. Material living conditions of children are deplorable in many countries, and every effort should be made to remedy the situation, but those conditions are not the only determining factor of juvenile crime since in the developed and some developing countries minors who are well fed, educated, living with the family, etc., sometimes contribute to crime far more than the less-privileged minors. What often happens is that with the help of their families they evade the juvenile courts. The problem is no longer that of 'children in trouble' but that of a post-industrial society in which minors are not what they were in the past. More frequently now juvenile offenders are brought before criminal courts when they have committed serious offences. This is the case *inter alia* in the USSR, Poland, Japan and some Arab countries.

Unfortunately the Congress indulged in a series of generalizations and contradictions, stating that the child was a child and a citizen; talking about the generation gap, claiming community support and that the justice required for juveniles has no legal connotation; that education begins at home; that there are age-shades of responsibility; that judicial intervention should be avoided; that the family should be encouraged; that juveniles in trouble should be provided with skills and experience in order to give them self-esteem, and so on. Briefly, without denying that many juveniles are in need of assistance, protection and care, juvenile crime is a growing problem. Some representatives were against the platitudes expressed but indifference, pressure of work or lack of information led to their acceptance without entering into the consideration of the role of young people in contemporary society.[18]

What is the meaning of trouble with the law? What kind of law? Should we put under the same heading running away, truancy, minor forms of vandalism, indecent behaviour, rape, bodily injury, robbery and homicide? Should incarceration be decided only for the protection of the minor and not of the community? Should we still conduct research into the causes of juvenile delinquency? Should the international community provide the means by which every young person can look forward to a life that is meaningful and valuable to himself, his community and his country without first instilling in him a sense of social responsibility when he has committed a criminal offence? It is not that minors should be judged as adults, but on an individual basis taking into account socioeconomic and political considerations as well as individual ones; age is not always a sure dividing line. If a NINCJO is to be created certainly age will not have the primacy granted to it by an obsolete criminology.

The erroneous approach has been maintained in the *Discussion Guide* already mentioned (A/CONF/121/PM.1). The subject of youth, crime and justice as a separate item of the agenda of the Seventh Congress was objected to by some of the members of the CCPC (among them the author) when the agenda was submitted at the 1982 session of the CCPC in Vienna. If a NINCJO is in the making the whole agenda of the Seventh Congress should be formulated within its frame and not as an ensemble of related items. The *Guiding Principles of Crime Prevention and Criminal Justice in the Context of Development and a New International Economic Order* included in the Annex to that document and based on those adopted at the Syracuse meeting of experts in January 1983, offer ample scope to approach the subject of youth, crime and justice in a more appropriate way.

In the *Discussion Guide* the old generalities are repeated without realizing that all three concepts (youth, crime and justice) are different in contemporary post-industrial society, to which not a single reference is made. No reference was made either to the increasing importance of youth in developed and developing countries, and their contribution to new types of values and aims. Without entering into details, suffice it to say that the assertion 'that the proportion of youth among the population will continue to increase for decades to come' is incorrect. A reading of *Population Distribution Policies in Development Planning* (1981) and *Projections of Urban, Rural and City Populations 1950–2025: The 1980 Assessment* (1982), shows that such will not be the case even among some developing countries. That youth is particularly vulnerable to ill-treatment, exploitation and neglect cannot be denied, but the same is happening to other groups in society. The fact is that criminal policies can no longer be based on repeated generalities originated more than 30 years ago mostly by Western professionals. The time has arrived for different approaches which need study and research – but not research into the causes of 'juvenile delinquency' which has barely been initiated. Like any other type of crime, youth crime must be related to crime victimization, probably the most important item on the agenda of the Seventh Congress. The correlation between crime and victimization shows that the old slogans of the prevention of juvenile crime should be forgotten. To begin with, the term is misleading and should be related to life expectancies in the different countries, without pretending to set a more or less uniform age limit for juvenile offenders. Another subject is that of the social and political responsibility of youth, particularly in the building up of developing countries. The need for a greater sense of responsibility was pointed out at Caracas by some delegations, among them that of the German Democratic Republic. Of course 'children should be saved', but adults should also be saved from atrocities committed by juveniles, now far more frequent than ever before.

In some Latin American, African and Asian countries youth is now participating directly in liberation movements to which the old slogans do not apply. Concerning justice, if a NINCJO is in the making the logical thing is to create one in which the role of age limits is not the main criterion for making distinctions. In other words, contemporary society can no longer be divided by age groups because age is only one of the factors to be considered. Otherwise we would need a variety of justices: one for juveniles, a second for young adults, a third for adults and a fourth for the middle-aged or elderly. The main problem is crime victimization, and to it all others should be subordinated. Fortunately, this has been understood by the Secretariat, which years ago started with the study of the abuse of power and the outlining of a NINCJO, and now brings forwad the main problem of the victims of crime. Put in a different way, criminology, criminal policy and related disciplines, without ignoring the offender, can no longer be centred around him, but rather around the victim. The main reason is that crime is becoming more and more a socioeconomic and political phenomenon in which behavioural approaches, although not ignored, are subordinated to more general aims among which protection is essential. This does not mean returning to the past but building up a new kind of criminal justice closely related to socioeconomic and political responsibilities.

It is hoped that the Seventh Congress will insist on maintaining the strict meaning of juvenile delinquency as it was adopted at the 1960 Congress, and that juvenile justice will become an integral part of the Guiding Principles of the NINCJO.

Capital punishment

Probably one of the first references to the convenience of studying capital punishment was made by the Howard League at the non-government organizations' meeting held in Geneva in 1956 (ST/SOA/SD/NGO.5). In 1959 the General Assembly adopted resolution 1396(XIV) inviting ECOSOC to initiate a study on the law and practice of capital punishment and of its effects on crime rates. Since then the General Assembly as well as ECOSOC have passed many resolutions on the subject.[19] What follows is a summary of the main activities undertaken by the United Nations on the matter.[20]

In 1963 the ad hoc committee discussed the question mostly on the basis of a study prepared by Marc Ancel. The main points were that capital punishment was still applied in many countries, that its deterrent effect has not been satisfactorily proved, and that in some African and Arab countries it was regarded as a public spectacle often attended by high officials.

In 1968 the Secretariat submitted a working paper on the subject to the European Consultative Group in Geneva, in which the results of the research undertaken in pursuance of these and other resolutions were examined. It was pointed out that there was an overall trend towards fewer executions, even towards a gradual abolition, but on the other hand certain offences of a political or economic character implying what was regarded as a serious threat to social order or governmental stability were gaining ground as capital crimes in some countries. It should be remembered that already in the 1960s the number of dictatorial regimes was increasing. The arguments in favour of capital punishment for economic crimes were based on the assumption that such offences involved deliberate planning, and that such a sanction would have the greatest deterrent effect. On the other hand it was claimed by others that economic crimes are not sufficiently grave to warrant the death penalty. Experience shows that since then economic crimes, some of them extremely serious, have been committed in countries with a central economy, and that capital punishment has not reduced them or the corruption often involved at high and medium levels. (It may, of course, be argued that without this penalty the number of economic offences would have been greater.) In any case, going back to the working paper, it was clearly stated that the research conducted was useless since it required too exacting an inquiry, and the resources available, particularly in developing countries, were lacking. It was added that the question of the death penalty was not one of research but of a moral, sociological and humanitarian character the roots of which are beyond the scope of research undertakings; and that whatever the results achieved by scientific research they cannot provide sufficient justification for the abolition or retention of the death penalty, a conclusion which is still valid (ST/SOA/SD/CG.2/WP.4).

Again in 1973 the Secretary-General produced a report on capital punishment (E/5242) in which the current situation on safeguards for the accused, the implementation of law and practices and other matters were analyzed. Summarily stated, the conclusions were that although the intention of the General Assembly resolution 3011 (XXVII) was gradual abolition, the data, not only those provided by governments but also by some prominent NGOs (among them Amnesty International), showed that the world picture was not really in favour of gradual abolition. It was specified that nevertheless the picture differs among developed and developing countries, the latter being far more in favour of retaining the death penalty. More specifically it was stated that 'the death penalty would still appear therefore to be regarded by a considerable number of governments as an efficient way of getting rid of certain types of problems whatever the experts say about the lack of deterrent effect of that penalty'; here again political aims were visible and seldom for the best. Concerning methods of execution, the report states that lately as supplementary means of frightening potential offenders in some countries executions were preceded by torture or beating or even beating to death the sentenced persons (p. 8). In any case public execution was still advocated as a deterrent in some countries developed or not. In some Asian and African countries it was still widely implemented at the beginning of the 1980s, sometimes as a public spectacle also attended by high officials of many sorts. As for the difference between the 'common' and the 'political' offender, the report states that apparently in some countries the latter are accused of being ordinary offenders and executed as such, and that in others the label 'political offender', was used to suppress any kind of opposition.

A reading of the report shows that, concerning safeguards, what actually happens is not necessarily what is prescribed by law. The protection against police abuse apparently depends on the power granted to the police by a given regime, and already in 1973, when the report was submitted, that power was out of bounds in some countries and 'extra-legal executions' by the police and armed forces were taking place. Political intereference with the judiciary was the rule and deliberately maintained. Although some references are made in the report to cases of judicial independence, the impression is given that in many countries, whether the judges were elected or otherwise appointed their independence was fragile. This fragility has been manifest in recent years in numerous countries. The proliferation of 'confessions' which were used by the judiciary in other countries to impose the death penalty should also be remembered. As the report states 'the administration of justice reflects often the power situation'. Concerning the number of executions, the paucity of data provided by governments is evident, and the report says that further inquiry in this respect is needed.

As was to be expected, practically no information was received from United Nations correspondents for the simple reason that all of them in democratic and non-democratic countries are appointed by the government, and very few will dare to say anything contradicting what is said in their government's reply.

Careful reading of the conclusions shows that capital punishment is often a way to dispose more or less legally, if that term may be used, of 'political' offenders or persons regarded as such. Concerning common offenders it is less used in most countries.

Capital punishment was part of the agenda of the Sixth Congress in 1980, under the item 'United Nations norms and guidelines in criminal justice from standard setting to implementation and capital punishment'. Previously, in pursuance of ECOSOC resolution 1745 (LIV) 1973 asking the Secretary-General to submit an updated report on the subject at five-year intervals, governments were invited in 1979 to provide relevant data in accordance with a questionnaire.

The Secretariat did good preparatory work, holding seminars on the subject and submitting a very interesting report. At that time the question of 'disappearances' had arisen as a governmental disposal procedure in some countries as well as 'summary executions' in others. Executions were also carried out by revolutionary groups of many sorts in some countries. By then the problem of capital punishment, already complex enough, was complicated by the kinds of execution mentioned.[21]

The Division of Human Rights submitted an excellent background report, *Human Rights and Criminal Justice* (A/CONF.87/BP/5,1980), in which the 'enforced or involuntary disappearance of persons' was examined. It was stated that the 'disappearances' were the result of excesses on the part of law enforcement or security authorities or similar organizations, often when such persons were subject to detention or imprisonment as a result of unlawful actions or widespread violence by those authorities or organizations. The Branch also submitted an excellent report, *Capital Punishment* (A/CONF.87/9 and Add.1980). After a descriptive reference to United Nations actions on the matter, an analysis was made of the answers received from governments as well as of the data gathered by the Branch itself, an innovation deserving praise since obviously government information, with some exceptions, was not as complete or reliable as it should be. The number of countries listed is 51; the number responding officially as member states was 22 . At that time there were 152 member states, so that 15 per cent complied with the request of the Secretary-General. None of the socialist countries provided data, nor did the USA, although some reliable information about them was gathered by the Secretariat. The result was that according to the answers only 22 countries throughout the world were totally abolitionist by law. Argentina, Chile, Cuba, Guatemala, Haiti and Paraguay did not provide information.[22] In the Cuban penal code, which came into force in December 1979, capital punishment as an alternative penalty may be applied for no less than 80 offences – including, according to article 98, helping the enemy in any way. In the new Chinese penal code, in force since January 1980, the number of offences punishable by death has been reduced, and in some circumstances execution may be suspended for two years and eventually replaced by imprisonment, but (and the 'but' is of considerable significance) article 79 permits the application of the penal code by analogy, that is, it may be applied to any act analogous to those described as crimes by the code itself. In this way the principle *nullum crime sine lege* is totally ignored.[23]

According to the report the assessment of legal executions for the periods 1956–60, 1961–5 and 1975–9 seem to be accurate, but no reference is made to 'extra-judicial executions' which already in 1970s were widely used by some countries. Offences against the government occupy the first place among capital crimes. In a number of countries capital punishment is used to protect the current form of government. In this respect it should be noted that in many penal codes or laws there is an identification between nation, state and government which cannot be justified.

The report adds that in view of the available data it is impossible to determine whether the process of restricting the number of capital offences has really taken place. Rather an opposite trend seems to emerge (p. 11). Public opinion apparently favours capital punishment in some countries. Owing to the complexity of the conditioning factors of crime the deterrent effect of the death penalty cannot be ascertained even with respect to common offences: in view of the abuse of the penalty it would seem that the same applies to non-common offences. The report states that one of the most discreditable effects of the sanction is the long waiting period before the penalty is confirmed or commented – which in some countries, such as the USA, may take several years. It is concluded that the Universal Declaration of Human Rights justifies the total abolition of capital punishment. the Branch's report aptly states that everything that could be said for and against capital punishment has already been said, and that to abolish or retain it remains a moral and political choice. Since United Nations criminal policy is reflected in the Declaration, the conclusion is that morally and politically it is committed to its total abolition. The report ends by stating that the death penalty constitutes a cruel, inhuman and degrading punishment.

As consultant to the United Nations on the subject for the Sixth Congress, the author made a brief exposition of the situation before the discussion started. With the exception of countries asking for total abolition and the few openly asking for its maintenance, the discussion was a good example of international ambivalence. Many countries expressed their deepest sympathy for abolition, but at the same time regarded capital punishment as necessary for the protection of what they called the state. More specifically the representatives of Nigeria, Sudan, several Arab countries, the Popular Democratic Republic of Yemen, India, Japan, Czechoslovakia, Bulgaria and the USSR also expressed their sympathy, but insisted on the necessity of maintaining capital punishment at least 'temporarily'. Most of the Latin American countries remained silent, the most significant exceptions being Ecuador and Mexico which were openly in favour of abolition. The Caracas Declaration does not contain any reference to the gradual abolition of capital punishment,[24] the impression being that it would not have been adopted if the reference had been made. Among the NGOs, Amnesty International made an objective and well documented intervention advocating abolition. The Howard League also advocated it, but with some reservations.

The draft resolution submitted by Ecuador, the Federal Republic of Germany and Sweden asking for abolition was eventually withdrawn in view of the overwhelming combination of comments concerning 'sympathy' and 'necessity'; the representative of Egypt played a leading role in defeating it. In sum, in spite of the numerous requests of the General Assembly, ECOSOC, abolitionist countries and the Secretariat, no action was taken.

The world panorama shows that the legal execution of capital punishment, where the penalty exists, is infrequent but in a number of countries has been replaced by 'summary executions' or 'disappearances'. Even assuming that not all the latter mean the physical disposal of a person, their number is big enough in many countries to justify the assertion that capital punishment is increasing. The impression given is that in some cases abolitionism *de jure* or *de facto* may be combined with 'disappearances': such is the case in Uruguay. There is little doubt that the proliferation of dictatorial regimes and their erroneous identification with the nation, country or state are strong conditioning factors for the growth of this kind of death penalty.

In some countries there is what is called 'death treatment' which consists in a combination of many hours of strenuous work, bad living quarters, poor food, lack of medical care, as much isolation as possible and whatever other measure is considered effective.

Practically all national laws refer to safeguards concerning sentencing and execution but in too many countries they are not applied.

At the 1984 session of the CCPC the discussion showed again that most of the members were in favour of retention of capital punishment. The exposition shows that for the time being the use and misuse of capital punishment as a legal sanction will neither be reduced nor abolished. A comparative study of all available data demonstrated that summary and arbitrary executions and 'missing persons' are parts of the problem of capital punishment. In some countries, while its use as a legal sanction is relatively minimal, its illegal use is frequent. Instead of dealing separately with each aspect, producing a plurality of documents, it would be advisable to deal with them as part of the whole. In this way the subject would be more easily understood and time, effort and money would be saved.

The abuse of power

Historically the criminal abuse of power became part of UN criminal policy as soon as genocide, crimes against peace and mankind, illegal detention or arrest, torture, cruel, inhuman or degrading treatment or punishment, 'missing persons', arbitrary or summary executions and other criminal violations of human rights were dealt with by the UN policy-making bodies. The criminal abuse of power is a long-standing problem which has been conveniently ignored by a large number of countries.

Realizing the extent and complexity of the illegal and criminal abuse of power, the Secretariat suggested that the subject be put on the agenda of the Sixth Congress in 1980. The suggestion was endorsed by the CCPC, and the subject was discussed first at the regional and interregional preparatory meetings of the Congress and afterwards at the Congress itself. Particularly constructive were the conclusions adopted at the ILANUD meeting held at San José in 1978, and at the interregional group of experts which I had the privilege to chair, at the United Nations, New York, in 1979. The main conclusions adopted were: that power may be used for legitimate purposes; that although all criminal abuse of power is illegal, not all illegal kinds of that abuse are criminal although illegality is frequently a conditioning factor of criminal abuse of power and therefore should be prevented; that the illegal or criminal abuse may be political, ideological, economic, industrial, scientific, etc., and even religious when it implies a regressive return to penal policy or sanctions; that with respect to economic abuse of power the expressions 'white-collar crime', 'criminalité d'affaires' and others, although still useful in some respects, do not apply to the wide area of economic crime in which bureaucrats, institutions, trade unions and other organizations now play a role; and that whatever its type the criminal abuse of power implies not only individual but also institutional or corporate criminal responsibility.

Concerning economic abuse of power, which often embraces financial, industrial, commercial and other related types, the following are the most frequent and often enjoy blatant immunity: bribery and corruption at high civil and military levels; monopolistic concessions or practices prohibited by law; illegal import and/or export of capital, goods, product, etc; false or unjustified loans; simulation or hiding of benefits, losses or any other financial or equivalent operations; abusive socioeconomic development, whether planned or not, particularly against national minorities or indigenous populations; simulation of prices or costs; illegal land speculation, concessions, transactions, exemptions and the like concerning urbanization or modernization projects, construction, expropriation, etc; false claims against government policies or programmes; tax evasion; currency frauds; illegal or destructive industrial action by trade unions, syndicates and the like; contamination and ecological waste; destruction or illegal exploitation of natural resources by public or private institutions, enterprises, etc; harmful food production and its import or export; export and/or import of pharmacological products which have been declared unsafe or dangerous; and the concession or blockage of public funds for illegal purposes.[25]

After reviewing the kinds of abuse of public power – a term which cannot always be identified with political or ideological power – in which terrorism should also be included, the group of experts expressed the view, in 1979, that its criminal abuse would not be adequately controlled at the national level except by (a) a democratic process which, if real, usually precludes it or at least makes exposure more likely, and (b) by the violent overthrow of the offending government by revolutionary force. It was added that neither solution was capable of totally controlling the criminal abuse of political power. As for the use of revolutionary force, it was pointed out, although it is not mentioned in the report, that in too many cases instead of bringing in a real democratic regime the one brought in is antidemocratic. Regarding the setting up of an international court to deal with some types of state or governmental abuse of power, it was stated that since it would not be able to enforce its decisions it would be of little use.

Analysis of the report and papers submitted confirms that the distinction between political and economic abuse of power is not always feasible, and that although called non-conventional offences there are all kinds of common crimes perpetrated in many cases by socially, politically and economically well-placed persons. Of most practical value were the conclusions that instead of expanding criminalization by promulgating special laws, penal codes should be drafted in a flexible way. Abusive interpretation can be prevented by adequate procedural guarantees and proper legal assistance; the inadequacy of the so-called penal systems to deal with the different kinds of the abuse of power was manifest.

At the Sixth Congress, the Secretariat submitted a very comprehensive report (A/CONF.87/6) in which the complexity of the abuse of power, whether illegal or criminal, and the types of offences and offenders involved were examined. The main points made were the pervasiveness and gravity of the criminality contemplated; the need for promoting a doctrine of collective responsibility with respect to any institution or corporation, whether public or not, without precluding individual responsibility; the increasing economic interdependence as well as the internationalization of business; the growing concern with consumer protection; the role of legislation; the need for better victim compensation; the frequent collusion between public and economic power; the need for further research and greater availability of reliable information; the improvement of the techniques of detention; the setting up of a flexible and wide-ranging system of sanctions; more respect for human rights; making public services more responsible; and support for non-governmental initiative.

The main points made by the Congress concerning the economic abuse of power were that generally national criminal justice systems were unable to cope with it; that in some countries the political and economic structures leave no room for individuals to acquire sociopolitical or economic power; and that there was a need for exchange of information and better policy formulations in economic matters. The discussion on the abuse of public power reflected a cautious attitude, mostly explained by the fact that a large number of delegations represented dictatorial regimes. The most significant points made were: the need for promoting ethical and professional values and norms; the need to intensify training programmes; and the need to ensure the protection of human rights and prohibit torture, political murder, abduction and 'disappearances' and suppress policies of colonialism, discrimination and oppression of the weak and disadvantaged. On the whole these points were satisfactory, but without suggesting that colonialism is justified the fact remains that in many newly independent countries the abuse of political power is a continuous source of crime committed with impunity, as has been attested by many UN documents. It is significant that no reference was made to the role of dictatorial regimes in the continuous growth of political murder, the condemnation of which has little value as long as those regimes exist.

The Congress adopted several resolutions which referred to the abuse of power. The two most important were resolution no. 7 and decision no. 5. The first recommended that the public should be made aware of the harmful consequences of the abuse of economic and political power, including that generated by the activities of multinational and transnational corporations; that effective strategies should be developed internationally, regionally and nationally to prevent, prosecute and control the abuse of power; that the UN should continue to gather, analyse and disseminate information about that abuse; that in order to combat it research and training should be developed; that civil and penal laws should be improved and prosecution beyond national boundaries made more effective; and that the UN should continue its work on the subject, and the possibility of an international agreement on illicit payments should be prepared. The recommendation conforms in many respects with UN criminal policy. The reference to multinational enterprises is very much to the point, inasmuch as quite often with the connivance of many regimes, most of them dictatorial, they play a role in the criminal abuse of power. The UN documents on multinational or transnational corporations are numerous, but probably the most significant as far as the abuse of power is concerned are those dealing with the code of conduct and their sociopolitical impact.[26] The drafting of a code of conduct is academic since its compulsory implementation, which is rejected, raises the still unsolved question of how this would be done. The role of multinationals, which is often beneficial, would be to a great extent limited by the effectiveness of a NIEO and by the suppression of corruption at high governmental and institutional levels. To rely, as the recommendation does, on the adoption of treaties, conventions, extradition and international agreements to reduce the abuse of power, is illusory when it is remembered that agreements concerning human rights are not observed by a large number of governments. A comparative study of 57 instruments[27] plus the list of ratifications, accessions and reservations with the list of countries the regimes of which are cited in the UN documents dealing with 'missing persons', arbitrary and summary executions, torture and cruel, inhuman or degrading treatment or punishment, *sine die* police or military detention and many other criminal violations of fundamental human rights will show that international instruments, codes of conduct and norms and guidelines will have a limited effectiveness especially under the dictatorial regimes which predominate.[28] The proliferation of international instruments is already being criticized, and in some cases they should be replaced by a list of offences constituting criminal abuses of power, subject to a compulsory extension of national criminal jurisdiction already mentioned.

The only thing to be said about decision no. 5 is that besides being partly a repetition of resolution no. 7 it consists of nothing but generalities. It refers again to exchange of information; reform of criminal laws; the improvement of existing machinery, and so on. The request for research on the etiology of offences and on the typology of offenders involved in the abuse of power as well as in the patterns, trends and dynamics of that abuse is no more than a delaying tactic. What would be the practical and even scientific result of investigating the causal process of the large and often changing processes of the abuse of political, ideological, economic, financial, commercial, scientific and religious power and of the many thousands of persons involved in order to set up a typology of offenders, a task which criminologically has little justification? How could these tasks be undertaken? The patterns, trends and dynamics mentioned are already sufficiently well established by UN documents, and by a large number of studies, some conducted by highly reputable NGOs. Although at its 1984 session the CCPC was supposed to discuss the subject, taking into account the document mentioned in note 28, once again lack of time prevented a full discussion.

Criminal justice

Since 1949 UN criminal policy has considered criminal justice as an essential part of its activities by discussing, at several meetings of the ad hoc Groups of Experts held before 1960, subjects such as detention pending trial, the abolition of holding persons incommunicado, arrest procedure, legal assistance, the use of detectors, and security police methods. Later, at the Fourth Congress in 1970, the judicial system as a corporate entity, community participation and the planning of criminal justice were discussed. In my lecture 'Crime and the Penal System', which was part of the activities of the Congress, I said that 'the only feasible and justifiable purpose of criminal policy is that of ensuring justice'.

At its 1974 session the CCPC considered the convenience of extending internationally national criminal jurisdiction; procedural delays; the strengthening of judicial systems; compensation to victims of crime; the suppression of commital proceedings in minor cases, and the reduction of criminalization by transferring some offences to civil or administrative jurisdictions (E/CN.57/19).

At the Fifth Congress, in 1975, criminal legislation, judicial procedures and related social control matters were discussed following, in some cases, a systemic approach. Among the conclusions reached the following should be kept in mind by policy-makers and professionals: the need for a long-term examination of the role of the subsystem of social control and of the evaluation of criminal justice systems as well as that of crime prevention; that criminal procedure, besides protecting human rights, should aim at the reduction of matters put through the whole penal process; that detention pending trial should be exceptional, and the range of sanctions widened; that the system of criminal justice should be planned, a task which cannot be identified with the multiplication of penal reforms; that the overrepresentation of the less privileged among those who are prosecuted or imprisoned should be abolished; that the historical error which has resulted in codes written for *lawyers* and not for the *community* should be rectified; that criminalization should be reduced to the minimum; that the independence of judges as well as a greater representation of women in the judiciary should be ensured; and finally, as a sort of all-embracing conclusion, that all countries should constantly re-evaluate their penal systems and criminal policy and, in doing so, keep in mind the role of coordination. The 1975 Congress has not been surpassed in the soundness and practical character of the recommendations and conclusions concerning criminal justice. How many countries have taken them into account in the reform of their penal systems? In this respect the world panorama in the last ten years is discouraging. The number of recalcitrant governments still introducing penal reforms without previous evaluation, planning and coordination is not decreasing.

At the Sixth Congress in 1980, the subjects of norms and guidelines in criminal justice and new perspectives in crime prevention and development were part of the agenda. The proceedings of the Congress show that by primary norms and guidelines were understood the provisions of the Universal Declaration of Human Rights and of the Declaration against Torture and Cruel, Inhuman or Degrading Treatment or Punishment as well as those of several covenants, especially the Covenant on Civil and Political Rights. Afterwards the transfer of prisoners, the need for guidelines in the treatment of prisoners in the community, the extension of criminal jurisdiction beyond strict territorial boundaries and the proper recruitment and training of judges were put forward as norms and guidelines. Although commendable, it would be difficult to maintain that there is an adequate parallelism between them and the principles embodied in the international instruments enumerated as a basic *modus operandi*.

The statement made by some delegations – mostly from Western countries – that progress in social conditions and penal practices goes beyond the SMR, and implying their modification, overlooks the fact that even in some developed countries the rules concerning accommodation, prison labour, remuneration, sanitary conditions, and other rules having a fundamental character are not applied in all their penal institutions. It is also overlooked that some of the new penal practices have not prevented the construction of huge prisons, euphemistically called 'facilities', the capacity of which sometimes goes well beyond the maximum laid down by the SMR. The rules have a world-wide purpose which cannot be subordinated to the progress accomplished in some Western countries which are not fulfilling some of the fundamental minima required by the SMR.

The assertion that the principles embodied in the UN instruments mentioned should be applied 'in the various regions and countries in a way fully consonant with their legal traditions and cultures' tries to justify the penal regression which is taking place in some countries in which cruel, inhuman and degrading treatment and punishment are carried out, by bringing back what is contrary not only to the instruments mentioned but also the principles and purposes of the Charter. Public decapitation, stoning, mutilation of hands (even if perpetrated by doctors, as in Libya), flogging and similar punishments cannot be justified whatever the weight of legal traditions. With the same kind of reasoning any country would be able to bring back inhuman, cruel and degrading treatment or punishment. What is more, it is now applied to those living in such penally regressive countries even when they have nothing to do with the tradition invoked. The question raised is extremely important in view of the growing acceptance of that penal regression in some countries, which is also against resolutions 6 and 11 of the Caracas Congress concerning torture and the prevention of cruel, inhuman or degrading treatment and, more recently, the draft of the convention against them (E/CN.4/1984/72).

With respect to the second subject, the proceedings contain references to the complexity of the phenomenon of crime at the national and international levels, to the convenience of knowing better the interrelationship between crime and development; that *per se* development was not responsible for the increase of crime – a conclusion already reached at the Second Congress in 1960; to the need to involve all relevant disciplines in dealing with the problem of criminality; that more research and analysis of the issues relating to crime and development should be undertaken, and that adequate attention should be given to the treatment of offenders as well as the transfer of prisoners. No doubt in view of the inertia of many governments all this may be regarded as necessary repetition of what has been said in the past, but it would be difficult to find in these statements any new perspective on crime prevention and criminal justice. The decision adopted on the subject reflects accurately what was discussed. It stresses the importance of the emergence of new types of crime, the need for closer consultation with member states and a systematic exchange of information; the need to promote international cooperation and technical assistance; that the UN should act as catalyst in promoting cooperation among developing countries – which it has been persistently doing without getting any reaction from many of them; that specific attention should be given by the CCPC to the question of the exploitation and traffic in persons; and that the capacity of the UN system dealing with criminal justice should be reinforced. Here again the requests, which are not new, are fully justified, but new perspectives are not clearly visible.

More recently the Secretariat, following a more practical approach, has been trying to formulate some guiding principles for crime prevention and criminal justice in the context of development and a new international order (A/CONF.121/PM.1,1983), and more courageously a NINCJO. The first were discussed at Syracuse by a group of experts in 1984, and in the same year a new draft as well as the reports of the regional preparatory meetings of the Seventh Congress were submitted, the latter at the last moment, to the CCPC at its 1984 session. Without trying to make an analysis of the guiding principles, suffice it to say that at the Asia and Pacific preparatory meeting (A/CONF.121/RPM/2,1983) 'most of the articles proposed could be considered appropriate and generally acceptable, although in view of the difficulty of the task, some further elaboration would be necessary'. Nevertheless the meeting endorsed in a general way the draft submitted. At the African interregional meeting (A/CONF.121/RPM/4,1983) it was stated that strong national penal legislation without a separation of powers was necessary for the re-establishment of social stability. Only the prevalence of dictatorial regimes in the region can explain such an amazing assertion. At the European regional preparatory meeting (A/ CONF.121/RPM/1,1983) the guiding principles were discussed in detail and as preliminary observations it was said that although the draft represented a valuable contribution it needed deeper consideration and elaboration; that the guiding principles should be more balanced; that they should be shortened to limit their scope, thus avoiding questions already discussed at previous Congresses; and that the vagueness or ambiguity of the concepts contained in certain principles should be corrected. Moreover, concern was expressed that the two years remaining until 1985 might not be enough to complete the work. It was recommended that the draft be considered by the CCPC at its 1984 session, a request which was not complied with in detail for the reasons given above. As long as a systematic exposition of what development means has not been adopted, it would be extremely difficult to say anything about the context of development so often referred to. The objection is greater with respect to the context of a NIEO which has not even been outlined, still less formulated. In this respect the difficulties already pointed out in the report mentioned in note 10 have been aggravated. Since, as repeatedly stated, particularly at the Fourth Congress, criminal justice and development are two different things, one may ask why, without putting aside development and the NIEO, there is an insistence on elaborating a series of guiding principles in a twofold context which have not been properly outlined.[29] Will the Seventh Congress realize the incongruity of relating the Guiding Principles to the dual context of development and NIEO without first having a clear outline of the latter? The truth is that while concerning development its context may be understood – particularly if account is taken of the socioeconomic and political matters already discussed – the same does not apply to the NIEO. What we are facing is growing international economic disorder. As already stated the references frequently made to the NIEO are more rhetorical than factual. Among other questions, the following may be raised: what are its main elements? What is its context? Which are the coincidental and opposing aspects of the two contexts mentioned? And to what extent should the development of crime be taken into consideration in the analysis of the contexts involved?

The fact is that the formulation of any Guiding Principles or, for that matter of a NINCJO, demands the analysis of a large number of factors which up to now has not taken place. One may also ask whether, although closely related, the Guiding Principles of prevention do not differ in many respects from those concerning criminal justice, which should include what is still regarded as juvenile justice. If so, it would be better to formulate them separately. What is the meaning of 'Guiding Principle'? The analysis of the 47 submitted also raises the question if all of them should be regarded as such. Owing to lack of time the CCPC was unable to examine the matter, and decided that the ECOSOC should forward the text to the Seventh Congress for its consideration. In view of the heavy agenda of the Congress, the reduction of which was suggested by some members of the CCPC at its 1982 session, and the time at its disposal, the chances for an adequate discussion are slim, particularly as little, if anything, is known about the context of the NIEO. The best thing would be that after a general discussion on the text, the Congress decides to send the whole matter back to the CCPC for final formulation of the Guiding Principles either as a whole or separately taking into account the already existing main elements of development including that of crime, and dispense with the context of the NIEO unless by then it has already been formulated.

Victims of crime

Although the references made to the victims of crime when discussing other matters show that the problem was not ignored, again following the Secretariat initiative the subject has been included as one of the items of the Seventh Congress. Under the label of victimology the victims of crime have been studied in the past although mostly confined to those cause by conventional crime.[30] At present the question embraces individual as well as collective victims who are often not fully aware of their condition, and if they were they could not negotiate for compensation by direct contact with the offender especially when the offence is the sequel to a criminal abuse of power, the large variety of which has been described above.

As part of the preparatory work for the coming Congress the Secretariat has submitted an excellent account of the problems involved, in which specific reference is made to aspects which are generally overlooked by traditional victimology. The main aspects dealt with are: that special attention should be given to certain particularly vulnerable victim groups (for example, the aged, the young, the infirm and women); that large scale victimization affecting entire segments of the population is mostly the result of genocidal policies, arbitrary or summary executions, disappearances, torture and pervasive oppression and other kinds of criminal abuse of political power; terrorism that economic exploitation, especially in developing countries, provokes large and collective victimization, and that new policies of prevention and redress are needed. As preventive measures the adoption of codes of conduct and other guidelines and intercountry cooperation are mentioned. Finally, a series of references is made to the studies initiated on the subject by UN institutes and other organizations.[31]

At the European regional preparatory meeting already cited it was stated that more scientific research was needed in the field of victimology; mention was made of the United Nations Voluntary Fund for the Victims of Torture (whose jurisdiction could be expanded, and whose creation deserves full praise and unfortunately shows that when compared with the past the second part of the twentieth century shows a barbaric regression); that compensation ought to be provided in some cases by the state; that the principle of equality should apply to victims of all crimes, regardless of their financial needs; that greater and more effective participation should be accorded to victims in criminal proceedings; that in some legislation payment of compensation to the victim has been made a prerequisite for granting a conditional sentence, while in other cases special funds have been created with part of the money earned by the offender during his imprisonment, from the collection of fines or from other state funds; and finally, it was stressed that financial compensation was not enough and free treatment for injured victims, social assistance and other measures were recommended.

At the Asia and Pacific regional preparatory meeting the growing spectrum of crime victimization was also examined, and specific references were made to victimization resulting from the misuse and abuse of public power; to the organization of programmes to include victims as partners in the adjudication process; and to the role that some traditional institutions may play in the settling of disputes and consequently in preventing victimization.[32]

The last discussion on the subject took place at the Interregional Preparatory Meeting for the Seventh Congress held in Ottawa in July 1984 for this specific purpose. Most of the participants submitted papers on the subject, a working group led by Professor Cherif Bassiouni was organized, and the discussion was preceded by an exposition made by the Executive Secretary, Mr Shikita.

The main points made were the following: a victim is any person who has suffered physical or mental injury or harm, material loss or damage or other social disadvantage as a result of a crime whether national or international; the term 'person' means an individual, member of a group or collectivity and also applies to legal entities and other organizations or to society as a whole; the rights of victims are based on the right to life, liberty, security and well-being; the duties of the State follow from legal obligations, collective responsibility and social solidarity; victims should have the right to redress from the offender, to compensation from the State, to assistance in their recovery, to fair treatment before the law, to access to justice and to protective and preventive measures; the rights of victims should not necessarily depend on the findings of criminal responsibility, and whenever necessary should be exercised by members of their family or any other person close to them; reparation is due at least for the loss of life, impairment of health, physical and mental suffering, loss of liberty, income, earning capacity, deprivation of property and intangible damage such as loss of reputation; victims of criminal abuse of power are entitled to full reparation from the State whose agents or employees have committed the abuse in the course of their duties; in countries where general social insurance programmes are insufficient the State should establish compensation programmes particularly when compensation due from the offender or any other source is unavailable; and State compensation should be provided promptly.[32]

Prevention

Traditionally the formulation of crime prevention policies and programmes has been flooded by well intentioned generalities, the implementation of which has always faced serious difficulties and yielded scanty results. Although UN crime preventive policy was originally under the impact of what may be called the 'generalist' approach, little by little it liberated itself from this influence and has now established a trend which it is hoped will be enlarged and taken into account by the makers of national preventive policies and programmes. The following is a short summary of the evolution of UN crime prevention policy.

In 1947 the *Preliminary Report on the Prevention of Crime and the Treatment of Offenders* (E/CN.5/30,Rev.1) submitted to the Social Commission, considered that 'antisocial behaviour is usually the result of hereditary and social factors', and that 'an investigation of the causes of crime is indispensable'. Accordingly the report makes the usual reference to individual emotional situations, family conditions and problems, lack of education, poverty, destitution and economic crises. All this represented an almost exclusively Western approach which, although historically and scientifically justified in some respects was in many others outdated. This approach was mainly concerned with offences and offenders of the 'lower classes'. Genocide; crimes against peace, mankind and security; torture and cruel, inhuman or degrading treatment or punishment; mass liquidation of opponents or dissidents and other criminal abuses of political power already well known; all these were regarded as outside a narrow concept of social defence. This point of view was maintained by *The Report of the Meeting of the Principal Organizations concerned*

with the Prevention of Crime and the Treatment of Offenders (E/CN.5/
104,1949) held at the Palais de Chaillot, Paris, in 1948 and attended
almost exclusively by European international organizations.

At the first meeting of the ad hoc committee of experts held
in 1949, the turning point from the traditional approach took place
when the causal approach to the study of crime was discouraged
at the international level. Concerning UN preventive policies and
programmes the implication was that a different approach from the
causal one was necessary.

At the Second Congress in 1960 the new approach was formulated
when the correlation between crime prevention and planning was
put forward as the basis of UN criminal policy. It was also pointed
out that development has an ambivalent character which may prevent
some forms of crime but create new ones. Unfortunately this twofold
conditioning effect has not always been taken into account by the
UN policy-making bodies, including the Secretariat which, by stressing the importance of development, created the impression that
criminal policy was virtually a part of it. This erroneous belief was
rectified at the Fourth Congress in 1970, and since then continuous
efforts have been made to avoid the swallowing up of criminal policy
by development policies which is unfortunately advocated by some
inside and outside the Secretariat, but certainly not by the Branch.

A further step in the right direction was made by the General
Assembly in 1972 when, by its resolution 3021(XXVII), it requested
the CCPC to report through ECOSOC on the methods and ways
likely to be most effective in preventing crime, including recommendations on the measures appropriate in such areas as law enforcement,
judicial procedure and correctional practices. By specifically referring
to these three aspects, the importance of criminal justice organization
was recognized as playing a significant preventive role which until
then had not been openly admitted.

In compliance with the mandate received at its 1974 session, the
CCPC organized four working groups: the first dealing with transnational and national crime; the second with correctional practices;
the third with law enforcement questions; and the fourth with judicial
procedures (E/AC.57/19,1974). The CCPC did an excellent job,
which unfortunately has not always been taken into account.
Although nothing specific was said about the abuse of power, it
was already obvious that in many of the problems discussed that
its prevention was most important in the prevention of crime.

At the Fifth Congress in 1975 the discussion on changes in forms
and dimensions of criminality and criminal legislation, judicial procedures and other forms of social control stressed the close correlation
between the appropriate functioning of criminal justice and the pre-

vention of crime which, until then, had been frequently overlooked because of the importance attached to a badly defined concept of development.

The most significant step in the right direction was taken by the CCPC at its 1976 session when, after asserting the impossibility of a crime-free society, it was stated that every effort should be made to keep it within tolerable levels. Unfortunately, due to various circumstances among which must be included preconceived ideas, the importance of the observation made as the *ratio essendi* of the future crime prevention policy was not realized by the CCPC or the Secretariat. No trace of a follow-up can be found in the subsequent sessions of the CCPC or in the preparatory work done by the Secretariat on the subject of new perspectives in crime prevention and criminal justice and development and the role of international cooperation.

The Caracas Declaration and recommendation no. 1 of the Sixth Congress in 1980 constitute a combination of traditional and innovative approaches which in some respects deserve to be retained, but not as the tenets of the prevention of crime required by contemporary post-industrial society. The need to review traditional prevention activities is specifically mentioned, but what is described can hardly be regarded as new and still less related to what was said in 1976.

In sum, if the prevention of crime is to be reasonably effective in the near future, a serious attempt should be made to ascertain as accurately as possible which are the guidelines to keep crime within tolerable levels. The task is not easy but the sooner it is undertaken the better. In any case there are elements to initiate it which, without making predictions, seem to be far more reliable than those discussed and adopted at the Sixth Congress.

Notes

1. For more information see issue no, 34 of the *International Review of Criminal Policy*.

2. The increasing gravity of the drugs problem was confirmed by the large number of resolutions adopted by ECOSOC at the session mentioned concerning illicit traffic, the need for more effective control, opiate and psychotropic substances, and so on.

3. For detailed information, see: *Exploitation of Labour through Illicit and Clandestine Traffic* (E/CN.4/Sub.2./L.460,1975); *The Question of Slavery and the Slave-trade in All Their Practices of Apartheid and Colonialism* (E/CN.4/Sub.2./AC/2/16,1978): *Handbook of Procedures and Criteria for Determining Refugee*

Status (Office of the United Nations High Commissioner for Refugees, 1979); Baroness Elles, *International Provisions Protecting the Human Rights of Non-citizens* (1980); and *Updating of the Report on Slavery submitted to the Subcommission in 1966* (E/CN.4/Sub.2/20 and Add., 1982). To these should be added *inter alia*, General Assembly resolutions 36/160 and 36/165, 1981, asking for the improvement of the situation of all migrant workers and the need for international protection of the human rights of individuals who are not citizens of the countries in which they live. For more recent ECOSOC resolutions on various aspects of inhuman conditions of refugees or displaced persons in general or in specific countries mentioned in the resolutions, see *Report of the Economic and Social Council* (A/37/3,1982). Concerning *Slavery, Slavery Practices and Apartheid* see the reports of the Subcommission on Prevention of Discrimination and Protection of Minorities, docs. E/CN.4/Sub./1984,23 and 25, the first referring to Mauritania and the second to existing practices in several countries of violence and coercion against women, female circumcision, domestic servitude, sale of children and exploitation of child labour, debt bondage and *apartheid*.

4. For further details of both groups of recommendations see the report of the Congress.

5. For detailed information see the reports of the European Consultative Group in the Secretariat series ST/SOA/SD/EUR. The whole collection was printed at the Printing Shops of Melun Prison, France, by courtesy of the then Director-General of the French Penitentiary Administration, Charles Germain. See also issue no. 12 of the *International Review of Criminal Policy* which, besides including the 'Inquiry on the Treatment of Abnormal Offenders in Europe', contains interesting contributions by Badonnel, Solms, Bradley and Blomberg and the report of the Third Congress.

6. Other studies were envisaged but not all of them undertaken, concerning other aspects of non-institutional treatment such as the payment of fines by instalments, forfeitures and loss of civil rights, and so on. For detailed information see issues 1, 2, 3 and 4 of the *International Review of Criminal Policy*.

7. *Deinstitutionalisation of Corrections and its Implications for the Residual Prisoner*, (document A/CONF.87/7.1980).

8. For details of the controversy, see Guy Care, *La planification* (1967), pp. 35–7.

9. Since, as repeatedly stated, the effectiveness of human rights is an essential part of development, the data put forward at

the above-mentioned meeting of the Commission based on the report (document E/CN.4/29,1983) are significant enough as far as this aspect of development is concerned. According to that report only 77 states have ratified or acceded to the Covenant on Social, Economic and Cultural Rights and 74 ratified or acceded to that on Civil and Political Rights which, in round figures, means that only 48 and 46 per cent respectively of the total UN membership were at that time parties to the Covenants mentioned.

10. See M. López-Rey, *Analysis of the Major Issues Involved in the Formulation of the New International-National Criminal Justice Order in the context of Development and of the New International Economic Order to Assist the Setting Up of Policy Options Relating to Crime Prevention and Criminal Policy* (1981). A summary of the report made by the Secretariat was distributed as the basic document at the Syracuse meeting in January 1983. Copies of the summary are available on request.

11. For details see M. López-Rey, *The Victims of Crime* (1984), in which a section is devoted to criminalization.

12. It should be added that since 1937, and mostly owing to Finland's initiative, the Northern Criminalist Association had studied the convenience of undertaking that comparison in Scandinavia. Several meetings were held in which Professor Veli Verkko played a prominent part.

13. In 1938 the League of Nations, with the cooperation of the IPPC, conducted an *Enquiry into the number of prisoners and measures to reduce it* which, judging by the results obtained, was far from satisfactory (Assembly docs. A.1938,vol.A/8–4,80).

14. The reader may make a comparison by looking at *Human Rights, A Compilation of International Instruments* (United Nations, 1983) and *Human Rights, International Instruments: Signatures, Ratifications, Accessions, etc.* (United Nations, 1983), and the numerous documents, some of them cited here, in which the 'indicted' countries are mentioned. The term 'country' refers to governments or political regimes.

15. Issue no. 9 was devoted to articles on juvenile delinquency as a work problem by ILO and as an educational and disorganization problem by UNESCO. The detection of 'pre-delinquency' was dealt with by WHO.

16. The attempt to extend juvenile delinquency treatment to young adults was put forward at the European Regional Consultative meeting in Geneva in 1952, when juvenile delinquency was discussed. The treatment of young adult offenders was again

discussed at the 1958 meeting of the Group. See ST/SOA/SD/ GEN/SR.1/1–15, 1953 and ST/SOA/SD/EUR/6/Add.1,1958 respectively.

17. See M. López-Rey, *Youth and Crime in Contemporary and Future Society*, Resource Material Series no. 4 (UNAFEI, 1978).

18. Unfortunately the report of the Congress does not reflect the objections made against the latitude given to the concept of juvenile delinquency.

19. For the period up to 1978, these are listed in *International Bibliography on Capital Punishment* (UNSDRI, Rome, 1978).

20. For supplementary information about resolutions see A/ CONF.87/C.1/L.1,1980, which contains the original draft resolution on the abolition of capital punishment submitted by Austria and Sweden to the Sixth Contress.

21. For more specific remarks see M. López-Rey, *Criminalidad y abuso de poder* (Madrid, 1983), in which a chapter is devoted to the death penalty.

22. The abolitionists by custom were the Holy See, Liechstenstein, Monaco, San Marino and Switzerland. The mixed countries were Australia and USA. The abolitionist by law were Australia, Austria, Belgium, Brazil, Canada, Cape Verde, Colombia, Costa Rica, Cyprus, Ecuador, Fiji, Finland, Iceland, Luxembourg, Nepal, Portugal, Sweden, Spain, United Kingdom, Uruguay and Venezuela. Other countries abolitionist by law did not answer; Argentina reintroduced capital punishment in 1974.

23. See Manuel López-Rey, *Los nuevos códigos penales de Cuba y China*, (National Institute of Legal Studies, Madrid, 1981).

24. The Secretariat had no direct participation in the preparation of the Declaration.

25. For details, see *Report of the Interregional Meeting of Experts on Crime and the Abuse of Power* (United Nations, 1979), and the working papers submitted, all in mimeograph form.

26. See particularly *Transnational Corporations: Code of Conduct* (E/C.10/AC.2/8 and 2/9 and 10, 1978–1979) and *Social, Political and Legal Impact of Transnational Corporations: Some Issues* (E/C.10/55,1979) in which crime is not considered.

27. *Human Rights: A Compilation of International Instruments* (United Nations, 1983).

28. One of the latest documents on summary and arbitrary executions (E/AC.57/1984/16) as well as *Political Killings by Governments*, (Amnesty International, 1983) reconfirms what has been said.

29. The complexity of the factors involved, which go beyond the

figurative concepts of development and the NIEO, is confirmed by much of what was said at the Congress on Criminal Justice Processes and Perspectives in a Changing World organized by the International Association of Penal Law, International Society of Criminology, International Society of Social Defence and International Penal and Penitentiary Foundation which took place in Milan in 1983. The Report was published in 1984.

30. This approach was still visible at the Seminar 'Towards a Victim Policy in Europe' (1983), organized by HEUNI. See particularly the recommendations which, although valuable, confirm the remark made.

31. For further references see A/CONF.121/PM.1 and note by the Centre for Social Development and Humanitarian Affairs as part of the preparations for the Seventh Congress (paper no. 5), both submitted in 1983, as well as the coming report of the 1984 session of the CCPC.

32. Concerning Latin America the reader is referred to the study *Victimización y victimología* (ILANUD, 1983), which was submitted to the World Congress of Sociology, held in Mexico in 1982, in which preventive policies, the extent of victimization, victims' characteristics, compensation and greater victim participation in criminal procedure are dealt with at the regional level.

33. For details see the report, in mimeograph form. In 1983 the Council of Europe adopted a Convention on the Compensation of Victims of Violent Crime.

4 Conclusions

The extent of crime, the basic element of UN criminal policy, is not known because of the paucity of government data. According to my own research based on UN data, the *International Crime Statistics* published by the International Police Organization, the national criminal statistics of twenty-five countries and the information contained in surveys, reports and other publications with respect to homicide, bodily injury, sex offences, burglary, robbery, theft and fraud known to the police in 66 countries with a population of 1,730 million, these offences amounted, in 1980, to 39 million.

At that time there were 160 independent countries with a total population of 4,500 million and one may ask whether the 39 million offences can be projected to the remaining 94 countries with a global population of 2,770 million. The technical objections are many, the main one being that although essential, population is not the only factor to be considered. My research shows that in the two groups of countries there are sometimes marked discrepancies between population and the amount of offences given, but also some remarkable similarities. Therefore, as a reasoned exercise it may be tentatively concluded that in 1980 the offences mentioned known to the police in 160 countries developed or developing, capitalist or not, was not less than 97 million, of which between 30 and 60 per cent were against property, not all very serious except for the victims who often belong to the lower echelons of society.

The figure may be regarded as high, but it represents only a relatively small portion of the seven offences. What about their corresponding dark figures? The dark indexes of each of them vary in every country. On the other hand the research conducted in some countries shows that the discrepancies are not always as marked as expected. Such is the case with homicide. The indexes of the dark figures of the other offences differ more widely, but if a general average dark index of ten is selected, which is extremely conservative, the result would be that in 1980 970 million should be added, making a grand total of 1,067 million offences.

Admittedly the figure is impressive but it is certainly not exaggerated. Conservatively estimated, the number of victims involved is at least twice as many, and the same applies to offenders. It should be remembered that the figures do not necessarily mean a different person in each case since the same person may be victimized more than once, particularly in large urban areas, and the condition of offender may occur in the same person quite a number of times.

What is the cost involved in the total amount of the seven offences? The answer is not easy since the term 'cost' should be understood to cover far more than the budgetary provisions assigned to the functioning of the penal system, including among others those resulting from victimization. After rather elaborate reasoning in examining the data gathered and as a conservative estimate, I decided that the world-wide average cost of each of the offences could be fixed at US$1,000. In doing so the average *per capita* income of a relatively large number of developing countries was considered. Certainly the average is higher in developed countries but they constitute a minority. Accordingly the minimal cost of the seven offences in 1980 would not be below 1,067,000 million dollars. In all probability it is considerably higher.

The figures may be contested, and in some respects they are vulnerable, but as a working hypothesis they can be maintained. Non-conventional crimes have not been included.

The main task of UN criminal policy is to determine the extent of crime as nearly as possible, and in this task other sources no less reliable than the governmental ones should be used.

The enormous extent of crime should never be used, as has been done by some, to advocate the abolition of penal systems on the basis that they have failed. In quite a number of cases direct understanding between victim and offender, under proper supervision, may replace judicial proceedings but we should not delude ourselves that such procedures can be applied to every crime, particularly those resulting from the different kinds of abuse of power, which often implies a sort of organized crime. Moreover, although important, the victim is not the only element to be considered. If development is properly understood and freedom, equality, dignity and security are to be protected, it is obvious that direct negotiation between victim and offender has only limited validity.

On the other hand it is obvious that penal systems are not what they should be in contemporary post-industrial society and therefore the formulation of NINCJO is becoming urgent. The Guiding Principles already examined may be seen in some respects as a step forward but certainly not as a substitute. In formulating the NINCJO consideration should be given to the question of criminalization, barely touched on by the Guiding Principles. It constitutes the point of departure to determine the potential extent of crime. the NINCJO should also reduce, if not abolish, all special criminal jurisdictions. Therefore military, economic, industrial, juvenile and other kinds of justice, jurisdictions or courts should be avoided.

The three main problems faced by UN criminal policy are the extent of crime, the formulation of a NINCJO and crime victimization. Although in all three the abuse of power plays a role, and development contexts should be taken into account, there are many other factors – already referred to in previous sections – which are no less important.

Concerning the extent of crime which, as a socioeconomic and political phenomenon, is inherent in any society, the first task is to determine the ways and means to establish what is the approximate amount that a given society can stand without being seriously affected in its development.

The task is difficult but there are already enough elements to attempt it. It should be kept in mind that traditional values and religious fundamentalism, although respectable, cannot play a primary part in criminal policy, so closely related to the preservation of human rights. Tradition and religion deserve to be taken into account, but within the limits established by the Principles and Purposes of the Charter and related Declarations and Conventions. In sum, crime is no longer a domestic problem but an international one in which all countries are immersed, and to the escalation of which many dictatorial regimes are contributing.

Domestically criminal justice may keep its own features, but these and all others should be in accordance with the norms set up by the NINCJO, the effectiveness of which demands the real independence of the judiciary and international cooperation.[1] Needless to say that order does not mean the organization of an international court of criminal justice but the adoption of an international criminal jurisdiction as an extension of the national one.

As for victimization, suffice to say that if crime is inherent in any kind of society the question arises as to the amount of victimization which may be regarded as bearable and whether or not compensation by the State is justified in every case. In other words while the necessity of assistance to victims cannot be disputed, compensation by the State raises the question of acceptance of crime as a risk which should be studied. What are the acceptable limits of such a risk? How should they be established? The acceptance of the risk has indirectly been taken into account in deciding that State compensation is due only in cases of violent crime and in accordance with some prerequisites. In this respect the European Convention deserves careful analysis.

These final remarks raise many questions but the conclusion is that UN criminal policy should be reoriented taking into account the growth of crime which, as stated, is its *ratio essendi* but barely known in spite of the efforts of the Secretariat. Historically the fragmentary approach to the question of the extent has yielded some results but the present situation demands a wider approach.

The CCPC should meet every year for at least ten working days and all the necessary documents should be submitted well in advance – the frequent delays are not always attributable to the Branch.

The Congresses should deal with only three subjects, as systematically related as possible, thus avoiding fragmentation; and they should be called Congresses on Crime Prevention and Criminal Justice. The reference to the Treatment of Offenders belongs to the past; its omission does not mean that offenders are going to be put aside. The name suggested corresponds to that given to the Branch in the 1970s replacing the Western title of Social Defence. The active participation of NGOs and professionals should be encouraged.

The functions of the Institutes, including UNSDRI, should receive as much support as possible from the governments concerned as well as from existing foundations or institutes interested in matters closely related to crime. The directors should be *de jure* members of the CCPC. Greater cooperation among them should be achieved, and in some respects they should work in accordance with the directives issued by the CCPC and the Secretariat.

Technical assistance should be increased. One of the ways would be to appoint more interregional advisers or create regional ones. The work performed by the present interregional adviser is gratifying enough to justify the suggestion.

The system of correspondents should be reinforced and made more effective; the cooperation of International Agencies, Regional Commissions and NGOs intensified. In other words, the sources of information and cooperation should be considerably enlarged.

In order to meet the responsibilities in UN criminal policy the Branch should be transformed into a full Division for Crime Prevention and Criminal Justice with adequate resources to fulfil them. The Department of Economic Affairs and the Centre for Social Development as well as all other bodies and services in which non-conventional crime is dealt with should cooperate closely with the Division, which should be in charge of the whole problem of crime.

Finally, it should be said that if social criminal justice is to become a reality the problem of crime, which is not merely one of development, should receive more attention than that given to it up to now by governments and the policy-making bodies of the United Nations.

Note

1   For the *Guidelines on the Independence of the Judiciary* see report of the 1984 session of the CCPC already mentioned.

Annex

In April 1985 a panel of eminent persons met in New Delhi and adopted a Consensus on the new dimensions of crime and crime prevention in the context of development which, in a summarised form, is as follows:

Crime constitutes a major problem of national and international dimensions which hampers the political, economic, social and cultural development of peoples; unbalanced or inadequately planned development contributes to the increase of crime; the forum of the United Nations has a significant role to play in order to combat crime at the regional, national and international levels; governments should give high priority to crime prevention and criminal justice in the context of development planning; attention should be given to the study and research of the possible interrelationships between crime and specific aspects of development and human rights; the impact of crime on disadvantaged sections of society should be studied, as well as organized crime including illicit traffic in drugs and drug abuse; criminal justice systems should be improved taking into account the need for their progressive humanization; non-governmental organizations should be encouraged to participate more actively in United Nations criminal policy and assist in its implementation; the Secretary-General is requested to undertake a comprehensive review of that policy, including the UN regional institutes, giving special attention to the coordination of relevant activities; in view of the growing magnitude of the problem of crime the Secretary-General is further requested to draw the attention of governments to the need to take effective measures in this regard; upon request the United Nations should provide technical assistance to developing countries and finally, the most effective guarantee against crime is the development of an educated and enlightened public opinion with the widest possible public participation in the efforts to combat this problem.

The Consensus confirms the main aims of UN criminal policy and deserves full support.

Index